A NEW ORDER OF THINGS

"When the tinkling of the bell on the Lyman Mill
re-echoed through the valley of the Blackstone,
a new order of things had begun."
—ERASTUS RICHARDSON, 1876

A NEW ORDER OF THINGS

How the Textile Industry
Transformed New England

PAUL E. RIVARD

UNIVERSITY PRESS OF NEW ENGLAND

HANOVER AND LONDON

University Press of New England, Hanover, NH 03755

Printed and bound in Spain by Bookprint, S.L., Barcelona

5 4 3 2 1

Developmental editor: Sarah Silberstein Swartz

Library of Congress Cataloging-in-Publication Data

Rivard, Paul E.
    A new order of things : how the textile industry
transformed New England / Paul E. Rivard.
        p.   cm.
    Includes bibliographical references and index.
    ISBN 1–58465–283–7 (cloth : alk. paper) — ISBN
1–58465–218–7 (pbk. : alk. paper)
      1. Textile industry—New England—History.
    2. Industrial revolution—New England. I. Title: How
the textile industry transformed New England. II. Title.
    HD9857.N36 R58 2002
    338.4'7677'00974—dc21   2002001698

Frontispiece: View of the Conant Thread Mill, Central Falls,
Rhode Island, ca. 1875.

CONTENTS

FOREWORD

For nearly two centuries, the order of things in New England revolved around coastal seaport towns, scattered farms, nuclear town centers, and a forest industry initiated by a request for tall trees to be made into masts for His Majesty's Navy. Life was controlled by the crop season, the run of spawning fish, and the rise and ebb of the tides. Although there was human enterprise, that enterprise was regulated by the rhythm and cycle of nature. In this agricultural environment, small mills located at the falls of water used waterwheels to grind grain and saw lumber. This small industry, along with the agricultural and maritime activities of farmers and fishermen, formed the economy of what we now know as New England.

Meanwhile, a political revolution was fought and won to make the English colonies in North America independent from the King and Parliament. Tall trees in New England were no longer recipients of the King's mark designating them for naval use. Then an industrial revolution, with ideas brought from old England, harnessed the waterfalls of New England for the twisting of cotton and woolen fibers into yarn. A new independence was gained. A new order of things began.

Instead of crops, it was now mills that flourished in the meadows. Factories sprouted in the fields. Farmers left the cycle of the seasons and settled for the rhythms of machines and the discipline of the factory bell. Life became more regimented. This regimentation eliminated some of the risks of a capricious Nature. Freedom to choose how to spend one's laboring time was replaced by routine. It was a new order of things, with emphasis on the word "order."

Few changes in human history were as dramatic as the advent of the industrial revolution in New England. It was a revolution of technology. It was a revolution in commerce, in transportation, in business organization. When at first work in the mills was done by families, it was not very different from the way people worked as a family unit on the farm or at another family business. Later, however, with the advent of the "mill girls" at Lowell, factory life actually liberated women by giving them a salary and an estate.

In the end, though, what was really different was the organization of repetitive functions and the gap in society that began to widen, from the time when owners and managers worked beside their mechanics on the shop floor to the days when they only left the board room for a ceremonial stroll to show the "hands" who was boss.

In *A New Order of Things*, Paul Rivard portrays the many aspects of the textile manufacturing story and assembles these parts into a new machine that transforms the world of classical New England. Rivard demonstrates his skillfulness and understanding of the way things work. He is a masterful mechanic in his own right.

Heritage Harbor Museum   Albert T. Klyberg
Providence, Rhode Island
March 2001

PREFACE

Writing this book has fulfilled a long-deferred ambition. Professionally, I have been involved with the history of the textile industry in New England for over thirty years. As Director of the Slater Mill Historic Site in Pawtucket, Rhode Island, from 1969 to 1974, I managed the restoration of the Oziel Wilkinson Mill and the Sylvanus Brown House, and the development of new exhibitions for the Slater Mill itself. Later, as director of the Maine State Museum, I continued my study of New England's textile industry by focusing on several major nineteenth-century Maine textile installations in the museum's "Made in Maine" exhibition. From 1991 to 1999, I served as director of the American Textile History Museum and continued my interests by helping to design and build the museum's facility and its core exhibition, "Textiles in America." When I stepped down from that position, I began writing this book, while serving as curator of technology for the American Textile History Museum.

All this experience and research in the field has led me to realize that there is currently no book in print that paints the story of the New England textile industry with a broad brush. Though there are numerous academic books on this subject (see my "Selected Bibliography" at the end of the book), none gives the fascinating details of the tale to a general readership. Early photography allows us an invaluable glimpse back in time. I was particularly interested in showcasing a large selection of rare photographs and paintings that provide historic images of the textile mills and their workers. Few of these have been published before, and almost none in color. The search to find the best images to illustrate the New England textile story became my mission.

One of the most important things I have gained in my three decades of research is an appreciation and respect for the New England textile workers, a population too frequently portrayed as faceless victims by those with political agendas. The stories of these ordinary people, the workers in the textile mills, have been too frequently lost amid a blizzard of facts and statistics, overlooked entirely by labor historians who present them solely as evidence of management avarice. On the contrary, these were real people who deserve the respect of having their stories told and appreciated without overriding motives. This book presents the story of the mill workers in words and in pictures. It seeks to recall and commemorate the ascendant period of New England textile manufacture, a century of momentous change which deeply affected the lives of the people and forever altered the order of things.

My other motive in writing this book is more personal. I remember as a child tagging along with my mother to the remnant sales in the woolen mills of southern Maine. There she bought yard goods for making clothing and mill ends and scraps "by the pound" to provide materials for my grandmother's braided rugs and my great-grandmother's hooked rugs. As bags of various cloths were gathered in the mill stores, I watched the wheels turning, listened to the heavy machinery, and smelled the acrid odors of woolen processing. I never forgot the experience. The sound of the many machines I encountered in my life as a curator always made me nostalgic for those familiar sounds.

But the story begins earlier, in the late 1870s, when my cousin Delianne Aubin and her family moved from their farm in St. Fortunat, Quebec, to Berlin, New Hampshire, to find work in the mills. Making a living on the farm in Quebec had been too great a challenge and, in the interests of monetary survival, Delianne and her parents—like many of their fellow French Canadian farmers—crossed the border into New England. There, Delianne found work among the many young women who became mill workers. She and her family left behind their French Canadian farming way of life, most of their friends and family, and all that was familiar—for what they believed would be a short time. They were never to return to their Quebec farm.

Delianne Aubin's uncle Telesphore Demers described the family farm in Quebec as "three miles into the forest, five miles without roads, nine miles to the store." Having served as mayor of St. Fortunat, he too eventually joined the migration to the New England textile mill towns. Though he himself did not work in the mills, he toiled for the owners of the mill in other capacities, no longer a free self-employed farmer.

Yet Telesphore had his dreams. He dreamed, for example, that his boys would graduate from college, an absurd hope for a French Canadian immigrant in 1900. In fact, his two sons, Odias and Phidlem (Delianne's cousins), did indeed graduate from the University of Maine. One served in the Maine State Legislature, a civil servant like his father, but an American of French ancestry in New England, rather than in French Quebec.

Living to the age of 102, Telesphore met his oldest great-grandson in 1950. Their conversation was in French, not difficult for his great-grandson who grew up as a French-speaking New Englander. Twenty-five years later, this same great-grandson would become director of the Maine State Museum and would eventually write a book on textile manufacturing in New England.

In New England today, the decaying mill buildings stand like shipwrecks, reminders of the passage of many families, like mine, who first came here to work in the textile mills of New England. Textiles are still being produced in New England communities today, but modern technology allows productivity without the need for acres of factory space and armies of workers. The old mills and factories stand idle, abandoned, recycled or demolished, while only a few of the many machines used in these mills survive as precious relics in museum collections. Thousands of spinning wheels and looms found in New England attics over the years are all that attest to an intense and vigorous past. Today these spinning wheels are icons, while the surviving homemade textiles have become treasured museum antiquities. The reality of the physically demanding labor of the textile workers has been replaced by a veil of nostalgia. And the spinning wheel has emerged as a symbol of preindustrial life, celebrated by antique collectors and museums as a reminder of simpler times. This book, then, is the story behind these artifacts and the story of the people who created and used them.

York, Maine   Paul E. Rivard
May 2001

ACKNOWLEDGMENTS

My research for this book began in 1969 when I was appointed director of the Slater Mill Historic Site, and it has continued intermittently for the past thirty-two years. The small but select Slater Mill library, assembled by the museum's first director, Daniel Tower, was invaluable to me, as was the significant collections of the Rhode Island Historical Society. There I was assisted by the director of the Society Albert T. Klyberg, and archivist Nat Shipton. My experiences during this period from 1969 through 1974 led me to a lifelong enthusiasm for the story of New England textile manufacture.

Work could hardly be undertaken without reference to the collections of the American Textile History Museum, known then as the Merrimack Valley Textile Museum. Here I received the advice and help of director Thomas W. Leavitt, who substantially created the museum during his twenty-seven-year tenure. I owe a debt to library director Helena Wright and chief curator David Jeremy. A gifted photographer, Steven Dunwell, worked with me in the early 1970s and produced a significant book on this subject, *Run of the Mill*, which was much on my mind as I worked on this volume.

As director of the Maine State Museum for fourteen years, I encountered new opportunities to study New England's textile history. The museum staff, particularly chief curator Edwin Churchill, assisted in many ways. Sharing space in the Cultural Building, both the Maine State Library and the Maine State Archives were incredible resources. Earle G. Shettleworth, director of the Maine Historic Preservation Commission, contributed his knowledge and enthusiasm for Maine history.

As director of the American Textile History Museum, beginning in 1991, I became quickly reacquainted with the museum's substantial library resources. In developing the museum's core exhibition, "Textiles in America," Clare Sheridan, library director, and Diane Fagan Affleck, chief curator, assured the accuracy of exhibition labels which in turn yielded a wealth of precise information used in the preparation of this book.

This publication was promoted by the enthusiastic support of several individuals beginning in 1999. The first and most significant sponsor has been Hugh H. Crawford, former chair of Stevens Linen Company and former trustee of both Old Sturbridge Village and the Merrimack Valley Textile Museum. It is fair to say that "Buzz" Crawford's early enthusiasm made this book possible. Important support came quickly from Whitney Stevens, former chair of J. P. Stevens Company, and Pauline Duke, current president of the American Textile History Museum.

After gathering my research notes and the ideas developed over the past three decades, preparation of the manuscript led me to retrace the steps of my professional career. Thus I returned first to the Slater Mill Historic Site where I received the enthusiastic support and help of director Gail Mohanty and curator Karen Conopask. I also went to the Rhode Island Historical Society where I was assisted by my old friend Al Klyberg and by the head of the library's graphics division, Jennifer Bond. At the Maine State Museum, Deanna Bonner-Ganter found some much-needed photographs, while Earle G. Shettleworth provided access to the Maine Historic Preservation Commission's rich photographic archives. Clare Sheridan at the American Textile History Museum afforded me access to the Osborne Library's unsurpassed archive, while assistant librarian Ann Cadrette efficiently provided some sixty images from the collection. Photographs of textiles in the ATHM collection were provided by curator Karen Herbaugh. Catherine Weller, assistant curator, was helpful, particularly in identifying some unusual dyestuffs found in some early blankets. Other help was provided by Eileen O'Brien at the Manchester Historic Association, Suzanne Olson at Gore Place and Cynthia Young-Gomes at the Old York Historical Society.

In addition to help from institutions, several individuals provided access to items in their personal collections or led me to new sources. In particular, I thank Robert M. Vogel, Marietta Binette, and Harland Eastman. Two principal readers noted for their scholarship in industrial history provided valuable insights: Dr. Merritt Roe Smith from the Massachusetts Institute of Technology and Dr. Richard M. Candee from Boston University.

Finally, I thank my son Christopher and also Sarah Stone for their help in providing new photography. Most notably, I want to recognize the contribution of my wife, Suk Hi, who long ago heard everything she ever needed to know about flax wheels and carding machines. Without her love and infinite patience with me, so little of what I have done with my life would ever have been possible.

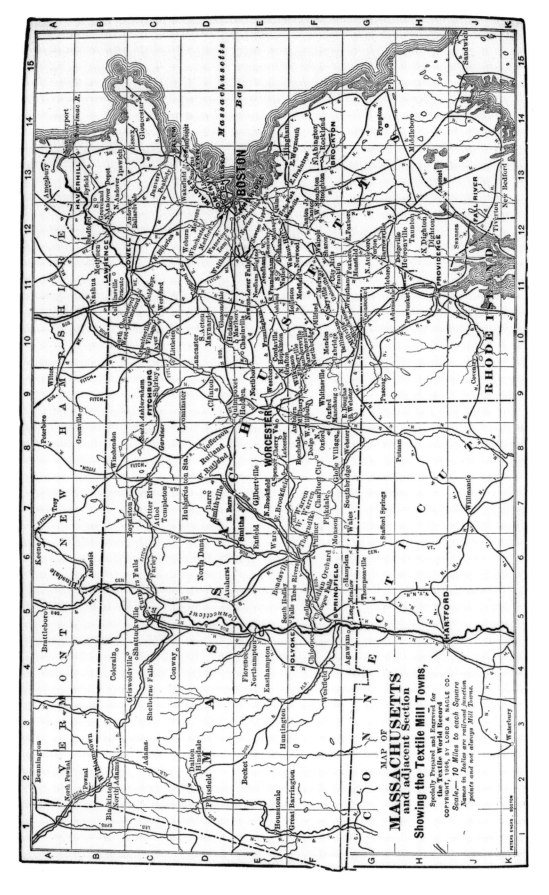

American Textile History Museum, Lowell, Massachusetts

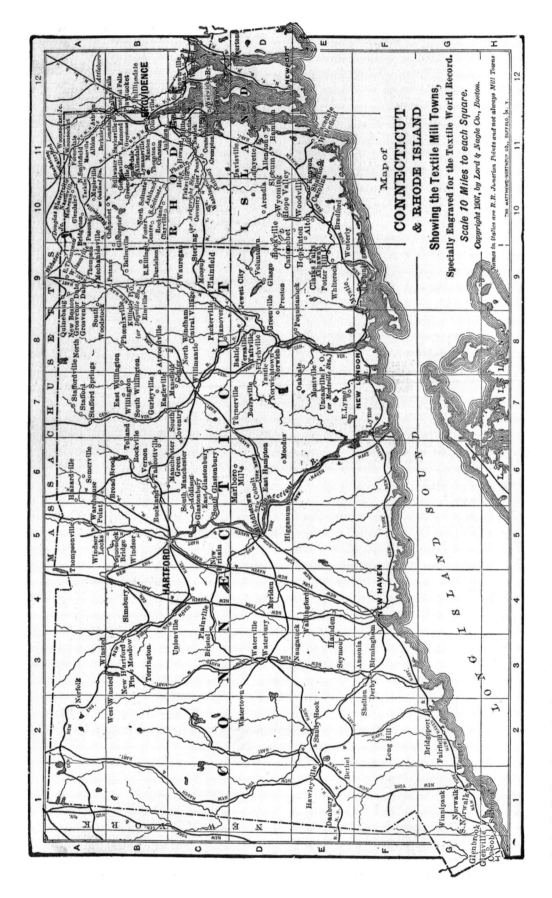

Map of

CONNECTICUT
& RHODE ISLAND

Showing the Textile Mill Towns,

Specially Engraved for the Textile World Record.

Scale 10 Miles to each Square.

Copyright 1907, by Lord & Nagle Co., Boston.

THE MATTHEWS-NORTHRUP CO., BUFFALO, N. Y.

Names in Italics are R. R. Junction Points and not always Mill Towns

American Textile History Museum, Lowell, Massachusetts

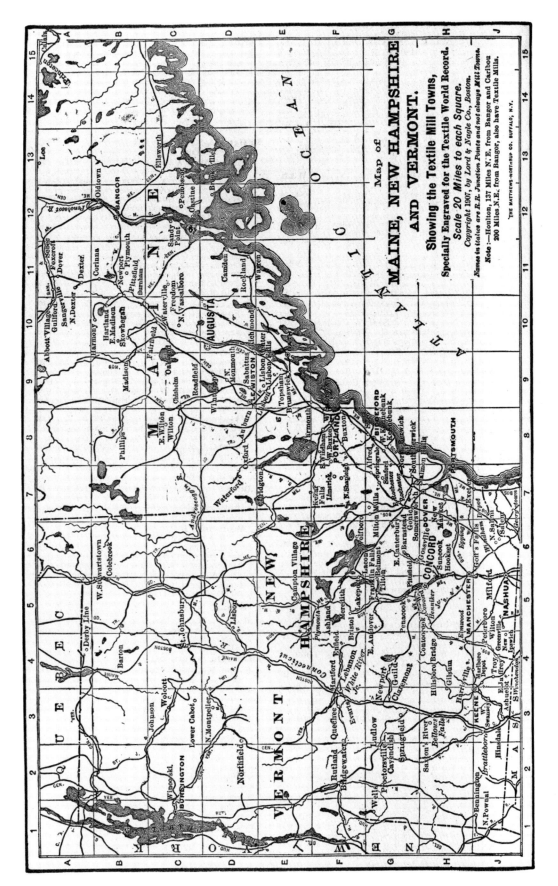

American Textile History Museum, Lowell, Massachusetts

A NEW ORDER OF THINGS

Chapter 1

Introduction:
An Overview of
the Textile Trade

In 1793, when Martha Ballard of Hallowell, Maine, decided to produce a piece of woolen cloth from her own wool, she knew she could make it more cheaply than she could buy it from Captain Howard's store at nearby Fort Western. But she also knew that this work would extend beyond the confines of her own "loome roome." Rather than producing it at home, she engaged the services of other local textile workers. Bypassing the use of her own spinning wheels, she had the wool carded or combed and then spun into warp yarn by Mr. Finney. She then took it to the home workshop of Peter Clark, where his family wove it into cloth. If the cloth needed to be dyed, this too was done outside her home.[1] In managing this production, Martha Ballard was in fact a manufacturer herself, producing cloth in her neighborhood—on the fringe of a much larger network of international trade. This was the typical state of textile production in New England at the end of the eighteenth century.

Textiles were actively traded commodities. Cloth was a necessity of life and when transformed into clothing, it was also a portable statement of status, wealth and fashion. In the eighteenth century, textiles were part of a worldwide marketplace. Products as diverse as coarse burlap for flour bags and as opulent as brocades for waistcoats and finer dresses required a range of textile choices from the coarse to the fine, from the cheap to the costly. In order to provide for this wide range of needs, textiles were bought, sold, traded, and exchanged through an international network that connected the whole world by shipping and inland trade routes. In eighteenth-century New England, as in all of America, more money was spent on foreign-made textiles than on any other imported commodity. A century later, the waterpower of New England rivers would

The tradition of domestic hand weaving is reflected by this ambrotype, ca. 1860. The weaver is making a rag rug, a home craft product. With the overproduction of factory-made cloth, large quantities of textile scraps became available for home weaving. *(Courtesy American Textile History Museum.)*

help create a new center of textile manufacture in North America.

Beginnings of the New England Textile Trade

When European settlers first arrived in New England, they encountered none of the natural resources, such as flax, cotton, wool, and silk, used for weaving cloth in Europe since medieval times. Supply ships arriving in the early seventeenth century brought sheep and flax seed, importing to America the fibers best known in Great Britain. The colonists also brought with them a fundamental understanding of both linen and woolen cloth production. This was enough experience to plant flax, raise and shear sheep, spin yarn and weave cloth, though perhaps not to the highest standard. This rudimentary domestic craft labor soon became the basis for a burgeoning textile industry in New England, despite Britain's constant attempts to inhibit production in the colonies through its mercantile policies.

Some settlers brought with them highly specialized skills. In 1643, for example, some twenty families came to Rowley, Massachusetts, from the wool-manufacturing section of Yorkshire, England. Through their initiative, the region's first fulling mill was built to assist in the finishing of woolen cloth. Later, just before 1720, a large number of Scotch-Irish linen workers arrived in New England and settled in and around Londonderry, New Hampshire, creating a center of high quality linen-making.

Though international trade in textiles was mainly controlled by merchants, domestic workers in rural New England also played a critical role in producing textiles. Along with later factory owners who copied equipment invented in Britain, those who worked from their homes were essential in the manufacture of textiles, especially in its early stages. This domestic activity continued, even after textile-producing factories were set up. Since the mechanization of textile-making processes was incomplete in New England's first mills and factories, the need for home-based labor became even greater as the industry grew. Here, the region's history of textile craft work in the home helped meet the challenges of the new machinery. Ironically, the most intense period of domestic textile work in the home actually followed improvements in machinery.

Wheels to spin flax fibers were common in New England homes through the 1820s and thereafter. In an age dominated by machines, these spinning wheels came to symbolize life at home in a simpler time. *(Source: William Hincks, London, 1783. Courtesy American Textile History Museum.)*

Local "Manufacture" and Imported Goods

Despite the international commerce of the textile industry, trade in cloth also took place on a very local level. Though quality goods were imported, homespun cloth was produced in rural New England. Here farmers grew and harvested the most common raw materials—flax and wool—and families in the area transformed their homes into workshops for processing these natural fibers into yarn. Although it had limited commercial importance, homespun cloth-making was widespread and economically significant for the livelihood of the people of New England. The extent of this home manufacturing led one Maine observer to note in the 1820s that cloth was "an important manufacture . . . conducted chiefly in private families; and it is well known that it is confined almost wholly to the female part of the families, to whom other modes of profitable employment are generally not open . . . and a large part of whom, without this manufacture, would probably have the opportunity to contribute but little to the general wealth of the state."[2]

Spinning and weaving had long been considered women's work—and with it came a certain amount of economic freedom. Though the work was often drudgery, it eventually led women out of the household and provided them with independently earned cash. Later, when home industry was replaced by factory work, young women left their parents' households for urban centers to earn their own incomes.

Even at the homespun level, there was considerable specialization and much house-to-house bartering—a variety of commerce at a grassroots level. Those who produced the cloth ranged from semi-skilled labor to highly professional skilled workers. Skill levels differentiated producers and the products. Many tools, like hand looms, were limited to those who owned houses large enough to accommodate them. The actual spinners and weavers who used the tools were often not the owners of the equipment, nor of the raw materials—nor were they the owners of the houses that served as workplaces. Though some family members depended on this work for their livelihood, textiles "made in families" made no one rich. For some, spinning and weaving was a job performed outside the home in exchange for room and board. Some homemade products found their way into the marketplace from

(Facing page top) Despite the dramatic rise of factory processes in the nineteenth century, the age of homespun actually continued for decades. In this image, photographed in Center Lovell, Maine, skeins of spun and dyed woolen yarn are being wound on spools to prepare for the weaving process, ca. 1900. (Courtesy Maine State Museum.)

(Facing page bottom) Hand weaving survived longest in rural areas such as the St. John Valley in northern Maine, where this photograph was taken, ca. 1880. (Courtesy Maine State Museum.)

(Above) Large domestic tools such as wooden hand looms were often dismantled when not in use. This early nineteenth-century loom features parts that have been numbered with matching sets of Roman numerals to allow for easy reassembly. (Photo by Anton Grassl. Courtesy American Textile History Museum.)

the bottom up. Exchanged at local stores, low-priced goods like bed ticking and tow-cloth were circulated to other households where no cloth was produced.

Despite abundant production, New England domestic cloth could not compete with fine imported products. Farm families filled the local needs for low-priced cloths in New England, while finer goods continued to be made by professional craftspeople in Europe. Imported goods were preferred by those who could afford them. Since the high fashion of the eighteenth century fed an appetite for expensive and exotic fabrics, homespun was considered second-rate. The whole spectrum of imported textile choices was too large and the pressure of fashion too great to be satisfied by the limited range of local products. The domestic homespuns we find endearing today were seen for what they were: coarse substitutes for the elegant products of European craftspeople.

This "overshot" coverlet was made by Lydia Spofford in Kingston, New Hampshire, ca. 1740. Overshot designs could be made when the colored filling yarn was allowed to "float" over portions of the background weave. These designs were popular for bed coverings, such as this example cut to fit a four-poster bed. *(Courtesy American Textile History Museum.)*

Homespun was more commonly used in remote or frontier areas where the trade in imports did not yet exist, or where the purchase of more fashionable goods was simply not affordable. In the farmlands of New England, for example, few could afford the finer cloths. Later in the nineteenth century, when the daughters of farm families arrived to work in the new industrial cities and appeared on urban streets wearing their homespun country clothes, the most recent arrivals were easily identified and sometimes ridiculed.

For utilitarian needs, home manufactures soon drove out foreign competition from some markets. British consul Phineas Bond reported in 1789: "Among the country people coarse linens in Mass[achusetts] Bay of their own making are in such general use as to lessen the importation of checks and even coarse Irish linens nearly 2/3ds."[3]

Two Revolutions

Before the American Revolution, there was little collaboration between domestic manufacturers and city merchants. Then a continuing series of political decisions led to the colonies' war for independence from Britain, cutting their diplomatic and economic ties. Later in the 1790s, a continuing series of technical inventions led to another revolution: the so-called "Industrial Revolution." Both would change the world as New Englanders had known it.

The 1760s brought a series of "intolerable acts" to the colonies—the Sugar Act, the Stamp Act, the Quartering Act, and the Townsend Revenue Acts—each one showing the colonists they could no longer rely on trade with Britain. The colonists called for independence from the old country. Resistance to new taxes and duties on imported goods united farmers and rural manufacturers with merchants, and, as an unexpected byproduct, encouraged them all to promote domestic manufactures. Of course boycotts of British goods and "spinning bees" did not totally replace British cloth. The Revolutionary army was itself still clothed in uniforms of British-made cloth purchased through Holland.

Flannel was probably the most common woolen product in New England households. Requiring little finishing, this fabric was used for both clothing and blankets. Shown here are examples of flannel from the "Handkerchief" Moody house in York, Maine, believed to have been part of the trousseau of Susan Jane Preble. The salmon/lavender colors were derived from a species of lichen common in New England woodlands. Natural dyes were often used. *(Courtesy Old York [Maine] Historical Society.)*

But all agreed: reliance on foreign imports was a weakness which threatened the new nation.

In 1791, Alexander Hamilton argued in his *Report on Manufactures* that only by developing its own industry, including textile manufacturing, could the new nation be truly free. Merchants in many New England seacoast cities agreed with Hamilton for patriotic reasons. Perhaps they also had their eyes on the financial profit enjoyed by their English counterparts.

The years that saw the Intolerable Acts also saw the development in England of new spinning technology: the spinning jenny, patented by James Hargreaves in 1767, and the roller spinning frame, patented by Richard Arkwright in 1769. Textile manufacturing created new British wealth and power in the hands of English merchants. While New England wharves piled up with the products of new cotton mills, merchants led the way as America struggled to catch up with the unfolding Industrial Revolution. By 1790, when the first successful textile mill was established in Pawtucket, Rhode Island, this fledgling country was on its way to creating a second revolution. Knowledge and appreciation of machine spinning technology escaped from the owners of the Pawtucket Mill, just as it had from its birthplace, England. The first small mill grew into dozens of small mills, and the dozens grew to be hundreds of larger mills—until all of New England was affected by the promises of textile machine technology. By 1840, there were more than seven hundred textile mills in New England—and this was only the beginning.

Chapter 2

Extend the Mills: Spinning Cotton in New England

In 1790, the landscape of New England was in flux, but few realized what dramatic changes were actually in store. Only one cotton spinning mill then existed in the region. Not a year old, it occupied a small rented space at the waterfalls in Pawtucket, Rhode Island. This solitary mill with its recently imported technology would soon become an invasive transplant, sending runners out along rivers and setting the seeds of America's industrial revolution in the fertile spots of New England where rapids and waterfalls provided mills with power.

Pawtucket provided an ideal site for waterpowered mills. Here the waters of the Blackstone River descended through a series of rapids and cascaded into Narragansett Bay. Vessels passing from the bay, through Providence, could reach the head of tide at the base of Pawtucket Falls. The native population had named the place "Pawtucket," meaning "fall of water," and it had taken the European newcomers relatively little time to find a use for this source of power.

Mills already built to tap the waterpower at this time included several large ironworks serving the needs of shipyards, along with the usual complement of saw- and gristmills. Here, waterwheels powered bellows and trip hammers to produce a large variety of iron castings as well as forged items as large as ship anchors. Pawtucket was already a thriving center of "mechanic" work before Moses Brown drove into the village in 1789 with Samuel Slater, a young English immigrant. These men were destined to seal an agreement that would bring cotton spinning to life in America and, with it, the transformation of Pawtucket, the Blackstone Valley, and all of New England.

Before 1790, cotton was known but used only sparingly in New England. Bags of raw cotton were purchased to stuff pillows, make quilts, or pad up-

The dramatic waterfall at the head of tide in Pawtucket attracted mechanics and mill owners beginning in the seventeenth century, when forges and casting furnaces used this power to produce iron for shipbuilding. *(Courtesy Rhode Island Historical Society.)*

holstery. Occasionally the cotton fibers were spun into yarn for use in combination with local linen or wool. But by the 1770s, technology had fundamentally changed the production of cloth. Cotton, foreign to the environments of both England and New England, would now become the most important manufacturing activity in both regions. When machinery to turn cotton fibers into yarn was first developed in England, the consequences were dramatic. Machinery demonstrated the potential to increase productivity and save labor by substituting smart tools for craft skills. Technology held an intoxicating promise for merchants and entrepreneurs in New England as well.

New Technical Developments

Two types of spinning machinery were developed in the 1760s, each based on a spinning wheel process. Hargreaves's jenny operated on the same principle as the wool wheel. It was a two-step process: first drafting, and spinning, then winding up the spun yarn on the spindle. The jenny operator ran a number of spinning wheels at once, the spindles ganged up in one hand-powered machine. Though it increased productivity, the job was still labor-intensive and demanded skilled attention.

Arkwright's roller spinning frame, or water frame, also increased productivity, and, as bonus, it required no human strength and little or no skill to operate. This machine used a bobbin and flyer design, similar to that of flax spinning wheels. Because the process was continuous and required little skill, the Arkwright process had an immediate and dramatic effect on textile commerce. What it did require was the power provided by waterwheels.

By the mid-1770s, the production of cotton yarn in England was already at a factory stage. Manufacturers like Jedediah Strutt, Samuel Slater's British former employer and mentor, produced cotton yarn by the mile in multistory factory buildings. British manufacturers monopolized their new technology and tried to keep it a secret. Rising to the occasion, American merchants promoted industrial espionage.

Several spinning jennies were built in America in the mid-1770s, but in general the colonies were not yet ready to open factories. After the American Revolution, merchants in the new nation discovered the extent of their disadvantage. British merchants continued to flood the American marketplace with inexpensive cotton yarn and cloth. America had won the war, but dependency on British manufacturing seemed greater than ever. The daunting power of British industry was apparent with each cargo of goods arriving at American wharves. Worse still, many of these cargoes were delivered on consignment to small warehouse owners or retail merchants, undermining the old monopolies. Immedi-

ate efforts were needed to promote manufacturing in the new nation, an effort born of both patriotism and envy.

The First New England Spinning Mills

The 1780s brought several new developments to New England. These involved the work of recent immigrant mechanics with both private and public encouragement. In 1786, two Scottish brothers, Robert and Alexander Barr, came to Massachusetts and built the region's first Arkwright-type carding and spinning machines. Winning a two-hundred-pound prize offered by the Massachusetts General Assembly, these machines were kept on public display in Bridgewater, with the goal of inspiring the work of other American mechanics. The display, known as the "States Models," was a "show and tell" experience, not the start of a factory. The Barr

Components of Sir Richard Arkwright's water frame for spinning cotton, using spindles arranged in sets of four, as seen in an 1823 English engraving. This "bobbin and flyer" system was adapted from hand-operated flax wheels, replacing the work of human hands with a series of rollers. *(Source: Richard Guest: A Compendious History of the Cotton Manufacture, 1823. Courtesy American Textile History Museum.)*

The Arkwright-style water frame was soon replaced by "throstle" machines, named for the sound they made, in which spindles were driven by cords from a long drum. *(Source: Abraham Rees, Cyclopaedia. Courtesy Slater Mill Historic Site.)*

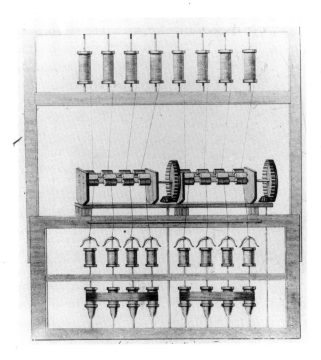

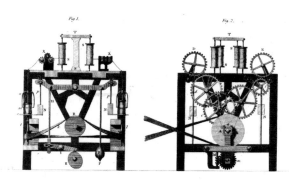

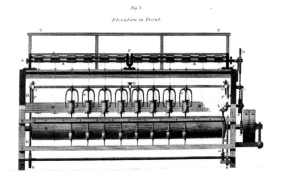

A spinning machine used in Slater's first mill (possibly the third machine ever built in New England), displayed at the Cotton Centennial Exhibition in Pawtucket in 1890. Now considered a national treasure, this machine is housed at the Smithsonian Institution. *(Courtesy Slater Mill Historic Site.)*

brothers collected their reward, purchased farmland near the Royal River in Yarmouth, Maine, and never worked in the textile business again. The models did eventually inspire the machinery used in the first successful cotton mill in America.

The States Model designs led to the first commercially successful spinning mill, not in Massachusetts but in Rhode Island. Here, merchant Moses Brown had determined to enter the cotton business. By 1789, several Rhode Island mechanics had made copies of the States Models and were attempting to run them. Daniel Anthony had built jennies for the Providence merchants Dexter and Peck, as well as an Arkwright water frame. In 1789, he moved these machines to a rented space in Ezekiel Carpenter's fulling mill in Pawtucket. Moses Brown bought the entire Pawtucket enterprise. Meanwhile, John Reynolds had built his own version of the Arkwright water frame in East Greenwich, Rhode Island. Moses Brown also bought this twenty-eight-spindle machine and had it carted to Pawtucket, where manager Daniel Anthony was put in charge.[1]

By August 8, 1789, the *Providence Gazette* reported that Brown had a thirty-two-spindle frame "after Arkwright's construction."[2] It was the original Reynolds frame to which an additional two sets of spindles had been added. This was the machine being run by Daniel Anthony in 1789, when Moses Brown first brought British mechanic Samuel Slater to the site of the Pawtucket mill.

Though Slater was disappointed by what he saw in Pawtucket, they agreed on a trial relationship. Slater would demonstrate his knowledge and get machines in operation by "using such parts of the old [machines] as would answer." In the months that followed, local woodworker Sylvanus Brown and metalworker David Wilkinson worked with Slater and Daniel Anthony to improve the machine built by John Reynolds. When Slater had proven his ability as a mechanic, it was agreed that Brown would provide the money to "extend the mills" to one hundred spindles.

Thus, by 1790, America had its first successful cotton spinning mill at Pawtucket, though it was a small beginning considering America's one hundred spindles were matched by England's 2,400,000. Moreover, the Pawtucket machinery required so many adjustments and improvements that it would be decades before the American industry could approach technical parity with Britain.

The machines built in Pawtucket were already yesterday's news in England. In the England of 1790, water frames and jennies were not the only successful spinning machines. A new machine, patented in 1779 by Samuel Crompton, was a hybrid of the roller spinning frame and the jenny. Appropriately called a "mule," this machine used the continuous roller technology of the Arkwright machine with the drafting and spinning process of the jenny. The first mule in New England arrived in Rhode Island in 1804, along with Samuel Slater's brother, John.

Operation and Management

The Pawtucket experiment indicated that there were two fundamental requirements for a successful cotton spinning mill: the ability to construct mills and machinery and the ability to manage them once they were constructed. New England millwrights were fully competent in building the needed dams, flumes, waterwheels, and mill structures. Textile mills differed from other common installations of the period. The portable textile machines were run by the same waterwheel, but the power had to be selectively turned off at each machine.

As the company of Almy, Brown and Slater prospered, it is not surprising that the Rhode Island mechanics who had helped build the first machinery were participants in the building of machinery for other mills. As with most products made in the eighteenth century, machines were custom built. As new cotton mills were opened, the job of building machinery for a particular mill was also launched. The first floor of the new factory was often used as a machine shop to build the machinery while the rest of the building was being completed. Since the machines were portable, it was not necessary to build them on site. But since the distinction between mill and machine was not yet clear, the tradition of constructing machines along with buildings continued for a long time.

There were other management challenges. Since

View of Pawtucket from the south, ca. 1820. From below the falls, products from the Blackstone Valley mills were taken downstream to Providence, Rhode Island. It was in this small community that mechanics first learned to run the new cotton-spinning machinery. *(Courtesy Rhode Island Historical Society.)*

Beginning with Almy, Brown and Slater's 1793 mill, the landscape around Pawtucket Falls reflected the growth of textile manufacturing, as seen in this watercolor painting, ca. 1812–1817. The bell tower can be seen above the bridge. Note on the right, the three-story "Yellow Mill" built by a group of Rehoboth, Massachusetts, investors in 1805. *(Courtesy Rhode Island Historical Society.)*

the operation of the machinery demanded little skill, it commanded little pay as well. Therefore, Slater's strategy was to use children for labor. This was not a particularly shocking concept in the eighteenth century. One of the first employees of Almy,

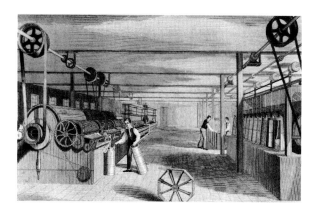

The interior of Almy, Brown and Slater's mill in this 1836 image, published in George S. White's *Memoir of Samuel Slater.* Although it was copied from an earlier English illustration, an important change was made to show young boys tending the machinery. *(Courtesy Slater Mill Historic Site.)*

Brown and Slater's mill was Slater's brother-in-law, Smith Wilkinson, who began tending the carding machine at the age of ten. Because spinning mills were built at remote waterpower sites, the search for labor helped create new communities: the mill villages. These would become an entirely new area of operational responsiblity for the mill owners.

The issue that most divided Slater from his partners was the strategy of running the business. Slater's idea was to produce a vast inventory by running machinery for maximum time and productivity. This approach was less appealing to those whose capital would be tied up in warehouses of unsold yarn. As they argued over deliveries of cotton to the mill, Moses Brown wrote to Slater complaining that he was "spinning all my farms into yarn."[3] Despite disagreements, cotton spinning was proven profitable, leading to a manufacturing stampede known as "cotton mill fever"—a time when "many a thrifty farmer and industrious mechanic embarked his all in mills and machinery."[4]

Chapter 3

The "Masheen": The Wool Carding Machine Comes to New England

When Cyrus Ballard of Hallowell, Maine, took four pounds of wool to the "masheen" in October of 1807, his mother, Martha, who had been carding wool by hand for at least twenty years, was making use of a new carding machine now available near her town. This was an improvement in textile technology that had dramatically changed the process of home spinning of wool for many of New England's home spinners.[1]

At the same time that Samuel Slater launched the cotton spinning mill in Pawtucket, wool-processing machines were also making their New England debut. As with cotton, this new technology was developed in England and successful clones required on-site assistance by a knowledgeable mechanic. Despite their similarities, the use and spread of wool technology followed a very different path from that of cotton.

When America's first woolen mill opened in Hartford, Connecticut, in 1788, the owners failed to make contact with the few informed immigrants from the wool manufacturing district of Yorkshire who were just arriving in the region. Despite improvements, such as the invention of the jenny and the carding machine, woolen production was still not successfully mechanized. Compared to cotton, woolen production did not appear to offer the same potential for profit. And skilled immigrants familiar with Britain's woolen industry encountered no entrepreneurial Moses Browns waiting for them at dockside.

The home manufacture of woolen goods "in families" was always a strong tradition—unlike its counterpart, cotton, which was rarely prepared in the home. Wool yarns belonged to the household, making the family the true manufacturer of the wool cloth. This had a profound influence on the spread and use of carding technology. The carding

The task of carding wool was slow and imperfect when done by hand. This early practice was demonstrated in a series of photographs taken in Center Lowell, Maine, ca. 1900. *(Courtesy Maine State Museum.)*

machine held the promise of speeding up the laborious process of hand-carding, while improving the speed of spinning and the quality of spun yarns. While eighteenth-century English wool technical improvements included the spinning jenny, the critical process was the carding. The rise of carding mills both assisted and promoted woolen production in the home.

The Rise of Carding Mills

Yorkshire immigrant Samuel Mayall was New England's pioneer in wool carding technology. Using machinery that was probably shipped illegally from England in parts, Mayall operated a carding machine in South County, Rhode Island, in 1788 and later at Bunker Hill in Boston in 1789. Samuel Mayall's mills were the first step toward creating a true woolen factory.

Other Yorkshire craftspeople soon followed, the most important of these being John and Arthur Skolfield who arrived in Boston in 1793. They were the first members of a large family of Yorkshire clothiers who came to New England and played a central role in spreading carding technology in the region. Starting with the production of woolen cloth using a jenny and a loom in Boston, the Skolfields secured sufficient sponsorship to establish an ambitious wool factory in Byfield, Massachusetts. Called the Newburyport Woolen Manufactory, it

Since carding machines were made mostly of wood, many mechanics were encouraged to build them locally for use in small carding mills. The engineering involved was not especially complex, but the quality of these machines was inconsistent, as was the carding itself. *(Source: Abraham Rees, Cyclopaedia. Courtesy Slater Mill Historic Site.)*

This two-cylinder carding machine, built by Artemus Dreyden of Holden, Massachusetts, ca. 1830, was found in the basement of the Hapgood Carding Mill in South Waterford, Maine. The machine is displayed in Lowell, Massachusetts, while the surviving mill and other carding machinery are on view at Old Sturbridge Village. *(Photo by Anton Grassl. Courtesy American Textile History Museum.)*

was incorporated in 1794. With the subsequent arrival of the other brothers, the Skolfields provided a formidable force of skill and experience held together by family ties. Using their diversified skills, the Skolfields engaged in a business that extended beyond carding to spinning, weaving, and cloth finishing.

By both producing and marketing cloth, the Newburyport Woolen Manufactory placed itself in direct competition with imported cloths, a difficult challenge due to the widely held belief in the superiority of English woolens.

A more immediate market for the carding factory still existed among the numerous homes where

woolen yarn was spun and cloth woven. While the more ambitious woolen factories faced uncertain prospects, the scattered home manufacturers of woolens, such as the Ballard family, proved to be willing customers for the machinery. Because of the advantages provided to home spinners, the carding machine in America enjoyed a life independent of the woolen factory. Located close to the work "in families," carding mills extended services of their equipment on a strictly local basis.

Not surprisingly, the technology of carding machines was not a secret for long and soon the Skolfields had competition. Operators of small sawmills, gristmills, and fulling mills quickly saw that carding

The interior of the Hapgood Carding Mill in South Waterford, Maine, photographed ca. 1900.
(Courtesy Maine State Museum.)

could be added to their small waterpower sites. The benefits of carding machines were immediately obvious and there was soon a great deal of competition to build them. The Skolfields left their large Byfield factory in 1798 and by 1801 Arthur Skolfield was building carding factories for others. Meanwhile, mechanics who had worked for the Skolfields building machines for their Byfield factory were already at work selling machines in western Massachusetts.

By 1810, the number of carding mills in New England grew to more than 700. This sometimes led to pricing wars, as reflected in an 1813 *New Hampshire Sentinel* advertisement:

Carding at Four Cents

The owners of the neighboring carding machines, viz. Those of Peterborough and Swansey, have been in the habit of underworking the subscribers the present season, not because they can afford to card for less than six cents a pound, but mainly to draw custom from the vicinity of other machines.

Therefore, the undersigned determined to commence carding on Monday the 9th Inst. Common Sheeps Wool for money in hand at Four cents the pound, for three months- trust at five cents, and to take pay in labor, or produce, or trust a year at six

cents the pound, and find oil for oiling at two cents the pound.

Packerville, August 2, 1813   B. Harris & Co.[2]

Only rarely did these small rural mills evolve into true woolen factories. Instead, they filled a niche of service to local hand spinners. Even with the development of woolen factories, it was the tradition of home spinning that kept rural carding mills alive well into the century. As late as 1879, for example, this fact was noted by a Skowhegan, Maine, newspaper speaking of the Stinchfield carding mill:

There has been a carding mill at this site for some seventy-five years and there probably always will be one here. . . . In the second story the wool is taken as it comes from the shears and run through a picker to remove dirt and separate hard bunches in the wool. Then it is run through the carding machine and comes out the long fleecy rolls which are spun for various purposes for which it is used. The rolls are then taken back by the farmer who brought them.[3]

Farm families near Skowhegan were making the same trip in 1879 that Cyrus Ballard of Hallowell made nearly three-quarters of a century earlier. Few pieces of textile technology had so great an impact for as long a time as the wool carding machine.

Chapter 4

Made in Families: Weaving at Home with New Tools

In the 1820s, the hand weaver's trade was still included in guidebooks listing a variety of common trades. This illustration is from such a guidebook. (*Source:* The Book of English Trades and Library of Useful Arts, *London, 1823. Courtesy Slater Mill Historic Site.*)

From 1817 through 1819, two teenagers, Mary Ann and Benjamin Mowry, earned money by weaving nearly one and one half miles of cotton cloth. Working at home in Smithfield, Rhode Island, they were paid between four and seven and one half cents per yard by the nearby Blackstone Manufacturing Company to make cotton checks and stripes, common cloths used for men's work shirts.[1] This cloth had about fifty yarns per inch and one yard required some eighteen hundred passes of the shuttle across a width of three-quarters or seven-eighths of a yard. The harnesses creaked into a new position with the addition of each yarn and the batten was beaten into place with a dull thud. This was the rhythm of weaving in the Mowry household. To fill their contracts with the Blackstone Manufacturing Company, there were over four million creaks and thuds.

Mary Ann and Benjamin Mowry were part of a large New England workforce of weavers—men and women—who worked at home weaving cotton cloth on a piecework basis. Their experience was common during the years from 1790 to the 1830s. For decades in the early nineteenth century, the production of cloth in America continued to be dominated not by mills, but by homes. Despite the great manufacturing advances underway, in 1820 an estimated two-thirds of cloth used in America was still "made in families."

Their handwork was made possible by power machinery in the region's first mills. Though factories were destined to make domestic textile work obsolete, from 1790 to 1830 mill machinery actually promoted at-home work. This became the era of most intense home manufacturing activity, with more cloth made in family homes than at any time before or after.

The industrial revolution, led by the manufac-

Before power looms, hand weavers often produced cloth in small workshops, which operated independently of spinning mills. *(Source:* Deissig Werkatten Handwerkern, *Germany, ca. 1850. Courtesy American Textile History Museum.)*

ture of textiles, was in fact no revolution at all but rather an evolution which lasted for generations. Some processes were mechanized long before others. When one step in manufacture was sped up by machinery, the steps just before and just after this mechanized process now became bottlenecks. The most notable bottleneck was in weaving, where mechanization didn't occur until a quarter-century after the development of spinning machinery. During the years from 1790 to 1830, the old hand looms were worked harder than ever before to keep up with the yarn produced by water-powered machinery, giving work to tens of thousands of New Englanders who labored in their homes.

Piecework

It was the manufacture of cotton cloth that did most to transform home weaving to a level of commercial importance. From the beginning of cotton spinning by machine in Pawtucket, the objective of merchants was not to produce yarn, but cloth. Perfection of the yarn spinning mill by Samuel Slater in 1790 began an avalanche of cotton yarn. To justify the continued production of yarn, his company, Almy, Brown and Slater, needed to turn it into saleable cloth.

Soon dozens of home weavers were hired to weave cloth for the Pawtucket mill. The cotton

This three-dollar note from the Manufacturer's Bank of North Providence in 1824 still features an illustration of a hand loom. Note that Samuel Slater was the president of the company bank at the time. *(Courtesy Slater Mill Historic Site.)*

yarns, spun by waterpower and owned by the mill, were sent to homes for weaving. As more spinning mills were built, the need for weavers grew. The supply of local weavers was soon exhausted and yarn was distributed to spinning centers farther away. This "putting out" of yarn by textile entrepreneurs to distant spinning centers of domestic weavers was a major production strategy.

At first, the mills contracted directly with the weavers. Later, shopkeepers became middlemen to get cloth woven in remote locations. In a cashless society, the shopkeepers provided their customers with a means to pay their bills by working off their debts. Weaving cloth becoming the payment for groceries. Soon the entrepreneurs themselves set up weaving businesses where many men and women labored at hand looms in workshop settings. When the Blackstone Manufacturing Company was contracting with Mary Ann and Benjamin Mowry, for example, it was also sending yarns to the operators of weave sheds in Warren, Rhode Island.

Much of the cotton cloth produced in New

The dim interior lighting of this hand weaving scene, from a photo taken in Center Lovell, Maine, ca. 1900, is a reminder of the difficulties faced by home weavers in the age before electric lighting. *(Courtesy Maine State Museum.)*

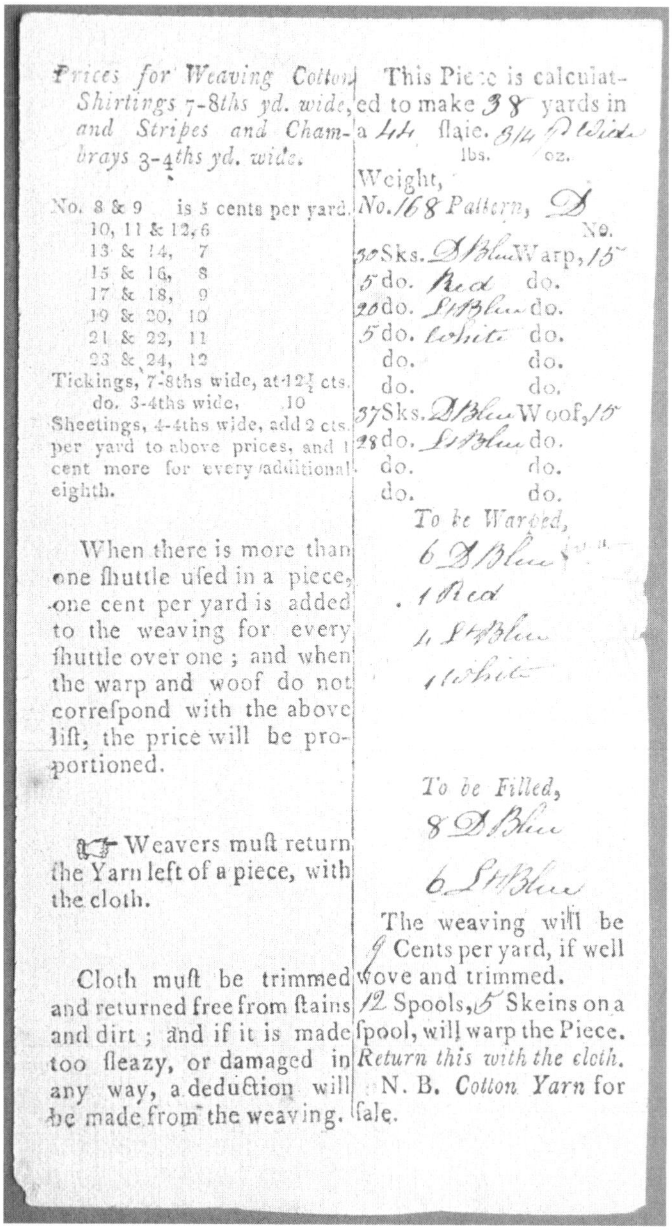

Prices for Weaving Cotton
Shirtings 7-8ths yd. wide, and Stripes and Chambrays 3-4ths yd. wide.

No. 8 & 9 is 5 cents per yard.
10, 11 & 12, 6
13 & 14, 7
15 & 16, 8
17 & 18, 9
19 & 20, 10
21 & 22, 11
23 & 24, 12
Tickings, 7-8ths wide, at 12½ cts.
do. 3-4ths wide, 10
Sheetings, 4-4ths wide, add 2 cts. per yard to above prices, and 1 cent more for every additional eighth.

When there is more than one shuttle used in a piece, one cent per yard is added to the weaving for every shuttle over one; and when the warp and woof do not correspond with the above list, the price will be proportioned.

☞ Weavers must return the Yarn left of a piece, with the cloth.

Cloth must be trimmed and returned free from stains and dirt; and if it is made too fleazy, or damaged in any way, a deduction will be made from the weaving.

This Piece is calculated to make 38 yards in a ... flaic. 3/4 ... wide.
Weight, ... lbs. ... oz.
No. 168 Pattern, D
No.
30 Sks. D Blue Warp, 15
5 do. Red do.
20 do. Lt Blue do.
5 do. White do.
do. do.
do. do.
37 Sks. D Blue Woof, 15
28 do. Lt Blue do.
do. do.
do. do.

To be Warped,
6 D Blue
1 Red
4 Lt Blue
1 White

To be Filled,
8 D Blue
6 Lt Blue

The weaving will be 9 Cents per yard, if well wove and trimmed. 12 Spools, 5 Skeins on a spool, will warp the Piece. Return this with the cloth. N. B. Cotton Yarn for sale.

Many home weavers produced cloth on a piecework basis using machine-spun yarns supplied by local spinning mills. The Blackstone Manufacturing Company sent instructions home with the yarn describing the pattern, the sequence and the colors to be used, and the yarns per inch, along with a yardage calculation and payment per yard. The instruction slip shown here was issued by the Blackstone Manufacturing Company in 1808. *(Courtesy Rhode Island Historical Society.)*

England homes differed from the traditional weaving of cloth for household use. No longer were the workers in business for themselves. Since weavers were paid by the yard for weaving yarns they didn't own, they were not independent producers of cloth, nor were they entrepreneurs. Instead they were laborers working on a piecework basis. Certainly yarns "put out" to homes added to the household income, but the pride and integrity often associated with pre-industrial life at the family hearth did not apply to this business. This weaving job was repetitive, no longer creative, and not much fun. One could say that weaving had become mechanical long before it was mechanized.

Power Looms

A satisfactory power-driven loom was not available until decades after improvements in spinning technology, and by 1810 weaving was already overdue for mechanical improvement. Power loom experiments had been made in England as early as the 1780s, but a quarter-century of further experimentation was needed before a really acceptable water-driven loom was in general use to weave coarser grades of cotton. In the first year of Mary Ann and Benjamin Mowry's contract with the Blackstone Manufacturing Company, the company purchased its first power loom.

Yet the era of hand loom weaving was far from over. The first power looms were limited to producing the simplest goods. The new looms introduced in Waltham, Massachusetts, in 1814 and in Rhode Island in 1817 could not duplicate the intricate checks and plaids then popular in woolen goods. The hand weaver's selection of different shuttles with different colored yarns could not be reproduced on these looms. Cloth produced in Waltham, and later in factory cities like Lowell, were plain "grey goods."

Thus, even while power-loomed goods were being advertised throughout New England, merchants in the 1820s were still hiring hand weavers. In the early decades of the cotton spinning mill there was plenty of work available weaving cloth for anyone

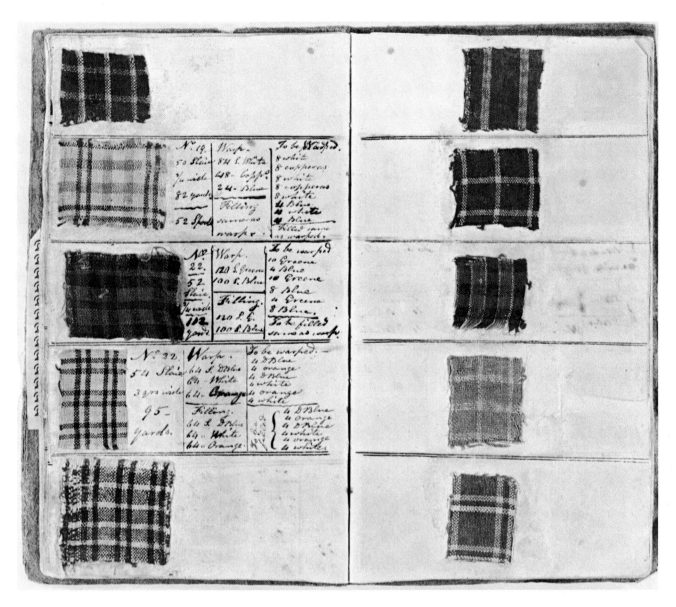

The Arkwright Manufacturing Company in Coventry, Rhode Island, maintained a sample book of more than eighty patterns offered by the company in 1815. Depending on the extent of the orders, cloth like this would have been woven by hand looms in family homes and workshops. *(Courtesy Rhode Island Historical Society.)*

willing to do it. When young women were needed to work in urban cotton factories, these mill "operatives" were often the same women who had already gained experience weaving long hours at home. For many of them, the task of running power looms compared favorably with the drudgery of working on the hand loom.

Better Spinning Equipment

Just as the carding machine had been a major encouragement to woolen production in mills, shops, and households, so were improvements in spinning wheels. No less than fourteen patents were granted for spinning wheel devices between 1790 and 1812.

This detail of a fly-shuttle loom shows the shuttle box, introduced in Rhode Island in 1790. This invention allowed weavers to pass the shuttle from side to side, using cords and boxes to catch and hold it. The first New England power looms were adapted from this hand loom design. *(Photo by Chris Rivard. Courtesy Slater Mill Historic Site.)*

Use of the "great wheel" for spinning woolen yarn continued well into the mid-nineteenth century. The efficiency of these hand wheels was greatly improved by the use of the carding machine. Note the number of carded rolags resting on the wheel waiting to be spun. The wheel is equipped with an Amos Miner "patent accelerating head." *(Photo from Center Lovell, Maine, ca. 1900. Courtesy Maine State Museum.)*

Detail of Amos Miner's "patent accelerating head." *(Photo by Chris Rivard. Courtesy American Textile History Museum.)*

The home remained the center of New England woolen production through the 1830s. Spinning activity in homes was encouraged by the development of jennies scaled down from factory size for home use. This "vertical spinning jenny" was patented around 1820. *(Photo by Anton Grassl. Courtesy American Textile History Museum.)*

Detail of the vertical spinning jenny, ca. 1820. *(Photo by Anton Grassl. Courtesy American Textile History Museum.)*

The production of higher-quality woolen cloth required "fulling" (felting process) of the cloth to shrink and thicken it by using large hammers, called "stocks," which appeared in New England mills as early as the 1640s. This nineteenth-century example of fulling stocks was used in Maine to felt cloth used on the rollers of paper-making machinery. *(Photo by Anton Grassl. Courtesy American Textile History Museum.)*

This ambrotype, ca. 1860, shows a woman posing with a wool-spinning wheel equipped with a version of Amos Miner's patent accelerating head. Hand tools for spinning wool yarns continued in common use well into the age of machine spinning. *(Courtesy American Textile History Museum.)*

The most important innovation was Amos Miner's "accelerating wheel head for spinning wool" patented in 1803. This device featured a small pulley system that added speed to the spinning spindle. Miner's patent head was a great success. By 1810, some twenty workers were producing between six thousand and nine thousand accelerating heads each year.[2] A wool-spinning wheel equipped with this head made possible the spinning of between three thousand and four thousand yards of coarse yarn per day. This increased productivity encouraged the continued use of spinning wheels and their mass production well into the nineteenth century. One manufacturer in Alfred, Maine, made some five thousand wool wheels a year at mid-century.[3] Meanwhile, jennies designed for use in factories were scaled down for use in homes.

Very little good quality woolen cloth could be produced at home without the help of a clothier and fulling mill. The fulling process used hammers and solutions to shrink the cloth and raise a "nap" of fibers. When sheared to a uniform surface, the fulled cloth served the demand for high-quality clothing. A fulling mill had been built in Hampton, New Hampshire, as early as 1642, and from then on such mills were frequently found alongside grist- and saw-mills on streams in rural New England.

The fulling mill in Alna, Maine, operated by Daniel Carleton, provides a glimpse into the weaving habits of the neighborhood. Over 3,600 yards of locally made cloth were finished by the Carleton mill in 1809. This total, however, was supplied by some 218 different customers. The yardage supplied by each household generally did not exceed twenty yards, and many accounts were for much less. The pieces brought in for fulling, pressing, and dyeing, ranged from two or three yards to about twelve yards. Lots of three, five, seven, and eight yards were common.[4] Obviously, home production of woolens was not necessarily intense, but it was widespread.

Chapter 5

Diaper, Tow, and Crash: Manufacturing Linen in New England

Before cotton became king, linen production was at its peak in New England. People favored this cloth because of its strength and durability. Before 1810, linen was the most solidly established and widely distributed of all the domestic handcraft industries in New England. But the invention of revolutionizing cotton-producing machinery changed the fortunes of linen. The difficulties in preparing and producing linen made this more painstaking manufacturing much less attractive to the New England textile industry—as well as to the people who carried out the work in their homes. The production of linen held its own in the decade following 1810, then sharply declined.

Linen was a casualty of the cotton-swamped nineteenth century, which favored the economy of the machine over traditional craft processes. Though less durable, cotton became a preferred alternative because it was produced at a far lower cost. Flax, the plant from which linen is produced, was possibly the first crop abandoned by New England farmers. By 1835, an article in the *New England Farmer* noted: "Of flax very little is cultivated, excepting that here or there a farmer raises a small quantity for thread in his family."

For many households, linen-making was just too much hard work. Growing and preparing flax was labor intensive and required considerable skill. Families soon lost patience with linen processing as a means of providing income when the newer, easier methods of cotton weaving and wool carding became viable. Preparing the flax fiber for spinning was a considerable task and spinning the refined flax required great of patience and skill. The production of higher quality linen had always been demanding. Poorly spun flax yarns or sloppy weaving produced obviously inferior cloth.

The labor-intensive processes of scutching and hackling are illustrated in this eighteenth-century English engraving. *(Source: William Hincks, London, 1783. Courtesy American Textile History Museum.)*

Producing and Refining Flax

The first tasks of linen manufacture fell to farmers, whose work began in the spring with the planting of the seed. The diary of Moses Davis of Edgecomb, Maine, tells this story. In April of 1773, Davis borrowed a neighbor's oxen to "harrow in" his flax.[1] The resulting crop was pulled up, roots and all, in late July. Then the seeds were removed to be used either as the next year's planting stock or as raw material for linseed oil. At this point the harvesting was over, but the processing of flax fiber was just beginning. Months of back-breaking work were required before the flax fibers reached the spinning wheel.

Flax is an annual plant, a member of the same family as hemp, sisal, and manila. Growing to a height of about three feet, the flax stalk is composed of a woody core surrounded by a ring of long, tough fibers running its length. These fibers are surrounded by a bark layer and glued to each other and to the stalk by a gummy substance. The process of getting the fibers out of this stalk and keeping them in good condition begins by forcing the stalks to partially rot. In 1774, Moses Davis, spread out his flax "to Rott" in mid-September and, no doubt, dried the flax and got it into the barn before the arrival of the snow season.

This rotting, or "retting," was accomplished by weighting down bundles of stalks in a moist area such as a stream, pond, or bog, or simply by laying out the fibers on a dewy night. Retting helps to disintegrate the woody substances, gums, and stalks

This flax-spinning wheel was made by James Gregg of Londonderry, New Hampshire, ca. 1780. *(Photo by Chris Rivard. Courtesy American Textile History Museum.)*

Flax fibers were drawn through hackles to clear away the outer husk materials and place the long fibers parallel to each other. *(Photo by Chris Rivard. Courtesy American Textile History Museum.)*

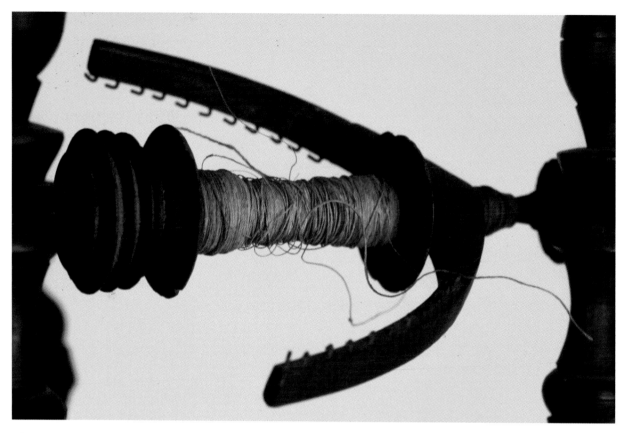

This detail of a flax wheel made by James Gregg, ca. 1780, shows the characteristic "bobbin and flyer" used on these wheels as well as cotton-spinning machinery. Both the bobbin (or spool) and the horseshoe-shaped flyer moved in the same direction but at different speeds. Thus, the fibers were twisted into yarn and the yarn wound on the bobbin in one continuous operation. This concept was central to the Arkwright-type spinning machinery introduced to America by Samuel Slater. *(Photo by Chris Rivard. Courtesy American Textile History Museum.)*

and to separate them from the fibers. Since the fibers are the toughest part of the plant, they are the last to be affected by the moisture. Still, the retting must be stopped and the stalks dried out before the fibers are damaged.

While the sowing, harvesting, and retting of the flax plants was most often physical work for men, the spinning of linen yarns was women's work. The task of preparing the fibers for spinning—braking, swingling, and hackling—could be done by men and women alike. Removing the fibers from the husk was a wintertime job that involved breaking up the disintegrating stalks using a variety of simple tools. First the outer husk was crushed under the force of the flax "brake." Then the loosened husk was knocked away using the "swingling" board and stick.

Because they made such a mess, the jobs of brak-

ing and swingling were usually done outdoors or in the barn. February was Moses Davis's favorite month for swingling. When properly handled, a handful of flax could be transformed into wispy hair-like fibers, and the stalk reduced to a pile of broken pieces on the floor. Swingling was the last flax process that occupied Moses Davis. The subsequent activities involved the women of the household.

Since the job of hackling—the "combing" of the flax—could be done in the home, women were often involved in this process. Martha Ballard occasionally did the hackling in her household. On March 18, 1786, for instance, she reported in her diary that she had "combed six pounds of flax." Hackling meant placing all of the flax fibers parallel to each other—essential for spinning—and combing out the remaining residue of dirt, stalk parts, and short or damaged fibers. This leftover material, called "tow," was used in the production of coarse cloth for grain bags and for the making of twines and rope, sometimes called "tow rope." Then the flax was ready for spinning.

The Business of Linen Production

In its heyday, linen production was an important specialized craft in Europe, particularly in Britain. Beginning in 1718, Scotch-Irish immigrants came to New England, bringing their skills with them. Taking advantage of these highly skilled craftspeople, the region began to specialize in producing quality linen. A large number of skilled craftspeople settled in Nutfield, New Hampshire, later renamed "Londonderry," which became known as a center for fine linens.

Many American merchants and consumers still preferred imported European cloth. In order to protect its linen industry, Londonderry sought government sanctions as early as 1731 to protect the use of its "brand name," already respected among linen products.[2] In 1748, a town meeting was called to plan how to keep foreign merchandisers from using the Londonderry name.[3]

The cultivation of flax and production of linens spread throughout the agricultural communities of New England. In 1810, an estimated one million yards of linen or partly linen cloth were made in Maine alone, 40 percent of Maine's total domestic cloth production. In addition, a great many of its sixteen thousand hand looms, found in an astounding 50 percent of its households, were being used to produce linen from locally grown flax.

In an era of expanding entrepreneurial energy, linen factories were launched in a number of Massachusetts towns, including Andover, Braintree, Walpole, Ludlow, Fall River, and Dudley. Of these, the Stevens Linen Company of Dudley was possibly the most successful and certainly the most enduring. Here, factory linen-making enjoyed a long, successful operation until the 1960s. Henry Hale Stevens —a son of North Andover's premier flannel manufacturer, Nathaniel Stevens—became interested in linen production during a visit to Ireland in 1845. Purchasing the Merino Wool Factory, an idle woolen mill plant in Webster, Massachusetts, Stevens imported European machinery and began a linen-producing operation in 1846.

The Stevens Linen business strategy focused on the production of coarse fabrics, avoiding competition with high-quality imports. Just as Nathaniel Stevens had concentrated his woolen business on generic flannel rather than high-end broadcloth, his son concentrated on basic utilitarian goods. From the outset, Stevens Linen produced a line of products from burlap to a range of bailing twine. The strength and durability of linen yarn and thread made it uniquely superior for most sewing needs, particularly for sailcloth and shoemaking.

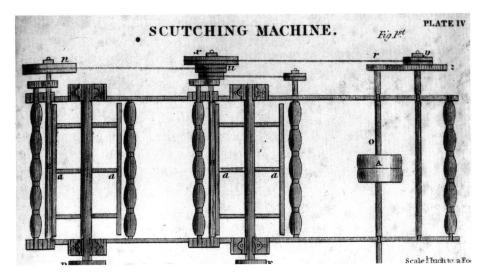

While the mechanization of cotton spinning quickly revolutionized the production of cotton cloth, the use of machinery in linen processing proved difficult. The simple machine illustrated here used rollers to break up the outer husk covering the flax fibers. *(Source: Abraham Rees,* Cyclopaedia. *Courtesy Slater Mill Historic Site.)*

The Stevens Linen Mill in Dudley, Massachusetts, as it appeared, ca. 1870. To the left of the smaller stone building is the original Merino Wool Factory. *(Courtesy Toltec Fabrics Inc.)*

The mill also produced fabric for towels in a variety of styles and grades. Designed to be nearly complete when they came from the loom, this toweling was woven to the finished product dimensions. In addition to "plain linen," Stevens Linen's products included fabric for "diaper," "drill," and "crash," a coarse fabric made with uneven and lumpy yarns. Except for the occasional weaving of linen for napkins, these products demanded less refined hackling and less complicated spinning than finer grades of linen.

Decline of the Linen-Producing Way of Life

In spite of Stevens's success, the nineteenth century saw the collapse of linen manufacturing. For investors, linen manufacturing became too risky, especially when compared to the high profits now expected in the cotton industry. In the competition for capital investment, linen production remained disadvantaged. With the phenomenal success of the cotton-based Boston Manufacturing Company in

Waltham and Lowell, relatively few New England investors were prepared to put their money into linen.

In the 1830s, linen still demanded a higher level of skill and experience, even though improvements were being made in the mechanization of the linen process. Eventually, each of the steps of braking, swingling, and hackling found its machine counterpart. These machines lessened the hand labor, but the remaining jobs were slow and laborious. The machinery was also wasteful, sometimes ruining a great percentage of the yield that might have been gained with hand work.

Rural New England workers gave up linen-making only grudgingly. Advances in the making of linen came slowly and, even when mechanization was introduced, hacklers, spinners, and weavers working in factories still clung to their "craft" traditions. Taking pride in their work, they seldom considered themselves "mill hands."

The decline of domestic linen production marked an important transition in New England rural community and family life. The old agricul-

This romantic promotional photo was taken outside the Stevens Linen Company in Dudley, Massachusetts, in the twentieth century. *(Courtesy Toltec Fabrics Inc.)*

tural economic base was eroding everywhere and the disappearance of linen became merely a sign of the times. The drudgery of flax growing and processing was a thing of the past. "So complete has been the change," it was noted in the 1860s, "that few persons under . . . thirty years of age, have ever . . . heard the buzzing of the flaxwheel."[4] It was the end of an era. Before the close of the nineteenth century, the rural farm activities of raising, processing, and spinning flax into linen fabric had already become a distant memory.

Chapter 6

Great Expectations:
Cotton Mill Fever
Creates Textile Towns

In the most rocky and desolate situations, avoided by all human beings since the settling of the Pilgrims as the image of loneliness and barrenness, amid rocks and stumps and blasted trees, there is a waterfall. Taking its stand here, the Genius of our age calls into almost instantaneous life a bustling village. Here factories are erected in this barren waste, and suddenly a large population is gathered. For this population everything necessary to the social state is created.[1]

Just as the American Revolution had jump-started American textile manufacturing, so the Embargo of 1807 and the War of 1812—both precluding trade with Britain once again—activated the infant American textile industry as a major economic and social force affecting the people of New England. What had begun as a local at-home industry suddenly became the impetus for creating new towns. Small mill villages spread like mushrooms during major textile industry speculation, initiating a period of rampant growth called "cotton mill fever."

First, small factories with machinery proliferated; then workers were needed to operate the equipment. Since most mills were located in lands along New England rivers and streams, which had a modest population or no population at all, finding labor became a major challenge. Since workers in textile mills had to walk to work—there were no commuters in the age of the horse—either the mills had to be placed among concentrations of people or workers had to be persuaded to move to the site of the mill. Cotton mill fever soon gave rise to mill villages specifically developed and sustained by the enterprising investors.

The master plan began with the development of the waterpower and the erection of a mill building. Next, owners set out to build or buy the machinery.

Beginning in 1806, Blackstone Manufacturing Company in Blackstone, Massachusetts, erected these stone buildings. Until about 1819, yarns spun in these mills were still woven in local homes. *(Courtesy Rhode Island Historical Society.)*

But none of these investments could be profitable unless a workforce was assembled. The first mills were relatively small; thus the labor needs were not extraordinary, averaging one hundred workers until the 1840s. But since workers were often accompanied by their families, housing for an entire community had to be provided.

Expansion of the Industry

The growth and spread of spinning mills was dramatic. Expanding outward from Pawtucket, cotton-spinning mills appeared on countless streams in New England, though nowhere more intensely than in the Blackstone Valley extending from Pawtucket upstream to Worcester, Massachusetts. This waterway and its tributary streams became the most densely industrialized river in the nation. The Blackstone Valley presented an almost unbroken strip of mills and factory villages descending from Worcester to tidewater at Pawtucket.

Along the Blackstone River, the greatest water-power and concentration of mills existed in the region of Woonsocket Falls. By 1844, there were some twenty-one mills in Woonsocket and sixty located between Slatersville and Pawtucket. Where the density of waterpower created the right conditions, smaller mills and villages led to groupings of small mills. The town of Thompson, Connecticut, had

seven mill villages within nine square miles. At Woonsocket Falls, owner James Arnold chose to build mills for lease, and the community became composed of various mills, each leased to a different company.

Many towns in this area began as small mill villages. Six separate mill villages eventually grew together to form the city of Woonsocket. Five of these villages—Social, Jencksville, Hamlet, Bernon, and

The "Butterfly" Factory in Lincoln, Rhode Island, was photographed in about 1875. On the second floor, between the first and second windows, one large stone was split, giving the appearance of butterfly wings. *(Courtesy Slater Mill Historic Site.)*

The mill town of Webster, Massachusetts, was commemorated in this engraving published in 1836. It was established by Samuel Slater, who named it after his political hero, Daniel Webster. *(Source: George S. White,* Memoir of Samuel Slater, *1836. Courtesy Slater Mill Historic Site.)*

The "lower" mill of the Greene Manufacturing Company at River Point, Rhode Island, photographed ca. 1860. *(Courtesy American Textile History Museum.)*

Globe—were clustered around the mills of single companies, beginning in 1810 with the Social Manufacturing Company, whose first mill was so small that it earned the local nickname "the Pistareen." In 1827, Globe Mills consisted of a thirty-six by seventy-two-foot cotton factory, a corn mill, the "Globe Store," two houses, and a barn.

The First Factory Villages

The early New England merchants sent their ships to ports around the world, while they themselves stayed at home in their counting houses in Providence or Boston. None of these men considered it necessary to sail off with their ships. Nor, when they began to invest in textile mills, did they consider living next to their factories. These mill proprietors ran their enterprises like ships; instead of a "super-cargo" onboard to manage their interests, now they

Beginning with the successful start of cotton spinning in Pawtucket in 1790, the Blackstone River became the most heavily industrialized river in America by the end of the nineteenth century. In congested real life, few scenes actually matched this romantic view of mills along the Blackstone. *(Courtesy Rhode Island Historical Society.)*

The "mule," as shown in this early-nineteenth-century lithograph, was a hybrid machine incorporating elements of the jenny and the Arkwright spinning frame. Introduced in Rhode Island by John Slater and Samuel Ogden in 1805, machines like this were being built in Pawtucket before 1807. Capable of spinning finer yarns, mules became a mainstay of higher quality Rhode Island–style mills. *(Source: J. R. Barfoot,* Progress of Cotton. *Courtesy Slater Mill Historic Site.)*

America's first successful cotton mill, built by Almy, Brown and Slater in 1793, still exists, as does the dam built to power it. The original Slater Mill, commemorated on a postage stamp, has been designated a National Historic Landmark and is operated today as a public museum. To the left is the Oziel Wilkinson Mill. *(Photo by Chris Rivard.)*

had mill "agents." Moses Brown and his relatives, for example, remained at their Providence east side homes and counting houses, communicating with their on-site manager Samuel Slater by letters sent back and forth to Pawtucket.

As the textile business in New England fell into the hands of a new breed of mechanic-entrepreneurs like Slater, whose "great expectations" depended on mills and machinery, this long-distance management began to change. For many small-scale manufacturers, their single mill site was their one "ship"

This photo of the Slater Mill and dam was taken about 1875. The Wilkinson Mill stands at the center with three building attachments standing over the mill tailrace. *(Courtesy Slater Mill Historic Site.)*

By the 1870s, the vicinity of the Slater Mill was already highly congested. The raceway seen in the foreground provided power to other mills downstream, including the nearby Wilkinson Mill. Many of the buildings shown here were built over the top of the flumes and raceways serving these mills. Water from the Slater Mill dam still passes under the Slater Mill in recently constructed flumes. *(Courtesy Slater Mill Historic Site.)*

of fortune, and so their presence "on deck" was required at all times.

The first cotton factory village was created in Rhode Island by Samuel and John Slater together with their Providence backers, Almy and Brown. First operated in 1807, "Slatersville" was the first of a genre of small mill villages destined to fill the river valleys of southern New England wherever there was a waterfall or rapids. At the site of Slatersville, 150 acres were purchased around a forty-foot descent in the Branch River. John Slater was the resident owner of the new community of Slatersville; he built a modest home near the mill, where he lived for the rest of his life.

Here, the fundamental ingredients of all mill villages were established: a waterpowered factory building (cotton-spinning mill), housing for the workers (two tenements), a home for the resident owner, a company store, and nearby agricultural land. Most mill villages of medium size, like Slatersville, eventually included a church, a bank, and a post office. Samuel Slater's biographer, George White, noted, "This village [Slatersville] is of recent date, having grown up with the manufacturing business, which may be considered as the parent of it."[2] Schools were established right from the beginning to provide for the incoming families. In 1812, the owners of Slatersville erected "a convenient brick building, to answer as a school house."

Cotton-spinning mills spread from Pawtucket

sometimes through the direct influence of Samuel Slater, his partners, and his workers. The expansion was slow at first, but more than twenty small mills can be directly attributed to Slater's influence. One nineteenth-century writer noted that "From 1791 to 1805 . . . all, or nearly all, the cotton factories erected in this country were built under the direction of men who had acquired their knowledge of the necessary machinery in Mr. Slater's employ."[3] And with each new grouping of factories came a mill town.

Life in a Mill Town

Slatersville was not a model for any other New England mill village, but everywhere the characteristics of a mill town were the same. In spite of an unstructured free-for-all environment of rapid growth, there was much similarity in the planning of mill villages in New England. The site was invariably near the natural fall of water or rapids that could be dammed up to produce the necessary power. The entire village was owned by the company and nothing could exist in the village without the company's consent.

Living conditions in the small mill villages appear to have been decent but crowded. The housing was not significantly different from the vernacular architecture of New England farmhouses of the period. They were, for the most part, multi-family detached houses that provided tenements for rent —for example, the two twenty-eight by thirty-six-foot tenements built at Slatersville in 1806. Not everyone found the mill villages tastefully situated as one observer wrote in 1844: "The dwelling houses of the village . . . are crowded together close to the road . . . their front doors open straight into the street. . . . The whole group has a slovenly appearance, and seem unfavorable to the habits of tidiness or feelings of home."[4]

The residents of the village needed sustenance. Some of their food came from produce raised on the company's own land by adult male members of the village families who did not work in the mill. Samuel Slater advertised in 1820 for a "Master Farmer, to take the lead of three or four men. One with a family to work in the mill would be preferred." The companies sometimes provided garden plots available for rent to their tenants. With houses located near the factory, workers sometimes went home for lunch. A strike at the mill in Salisbury, Massachusetts, in 1852 was precipitated when the agent unwisely abolished the ancient privilege of leaving the mill at lunch time.

A company store on the premises was another requirement. Since factories were often built in remote locations, the ordinary needs of the families had to be served by a store carrying food and other necessities. In a cash-poor rural economy, the store provided credit during the long intervals between the settlement of accounts, a system familiar to farming families. Little, if any, profit accrued to the companies from their store operations. A store was often run at a loss but was needed to hold on to the families it had attracted. Owners sometimes found this a burden. With an investment made to maintain the company store, owners expected their employees to patronize it and notices frequently reminded workers:

> Those employed at these mills and works will take notice, that a store is kept for their accommodation, where they can purchase the best goods at fair prices and it is expected that all will draw their goods from said store. Those who do not are informed that there are plenty of others who would be glad to take their places at less wages.[5]

As with so many company rules, enforcement was difficult. It is not likely that many good workers were ever discharged for shopping violations.

Mill owners continued to live in their villages, at least in the early decades. As owners of the whole village, these proprietors exerted great and often unappreciated influence on the village. An unwanted spirit of paternalism and moral authority often arose in the village.

Smith Wilkinson, Slater's nephew (who had tended his first carding machine at the age of ten), was the resident owner of a mill village established on the Quinebaug River in eastern Connecticut,

The Oziel Wilkinson Mill, built in 1810, is one of the best surviving examples of the many small cotton mills built after the Embargo of 1807 during the resulting rush to cotton manufacturing known as "cotton mill fever." The relationship between the Wilkinson family and Slater was close. David Wilkinson built the iron parts for the first Slater machines and Slater married Oziel Wilkinson's daughter, Hannah. *(Photo by Chris Rivard.)*

called the Pomfret Factory. Here, Wilkinson carried the mill village concept a bit further, creating an environment meant to serve as a positive force in the "reform" of families that were "often very ignorant, and too often vicious."[6] The Pomfret factory purchased one thousand acres of land around the mill. "The largest object of this company in buying so much land," Wilkinson recalled, "was to prevent the introduction of taverns and grog shops."

Spirits were banned from the mill village supporting Jedediah Tracy's mill in Troy (Fall River). "In order to keep out tippling and grog shops," Tracy wrote in the 1830s, "I have a clause inserted in all the leases given for building lots, that anyone selling ardent spirits on the same, forfeits the premises." When the "no spirits" policy was adopted, those workers who chose to stay had their debts divided into small sums, which they agreed to have deducted from their wages weekly. Rents were all payable weekly as well, that "no debts might be suffered to accumulate against the hands . . ."[7]

Mill owners often wanted to believe they were providing an environment beneficial to the families in the mill village. As Jedediah Tracy wrote: "It should be the first object of our manufacturing establishments, to have their superintendents, and overseers, and agents, men of religious principles, and let it be felt by the owners that it is always for their interest to support religion, schools, and all those institutions which promote good morals, and diffuse information among the operatives and their families."[8] To him, the mill village was to provide what he considered an "ideal" environment for his workers.

The Challenges of Mill Towns

There were problems facing the emerging mill villages that were issues for both the owners and the workers. On the large scale, the newly found opportunities in textile manufacturing were rapidly

This daguerreotype, ca. 1850, is one of many images documenting the much-admired Crown and Eagle mills in Uxbridge, Massachusetts. Together with its adjacent machine shop and worker housing, the Crown and Eagle site has long been recognized as a classic, and beautiful, New England mill village. Arson destroyed the buildings in the 1970s. *(Courtesy American Textile History Museum.)*

absorbing capital and creating an economy short on diversity. Rhode Island, in particular, was turning into a one-industry region. On the more local level, the capital invested in mill villages was often modest and the entrepreneurs could not withstand serious economic downturns. In bad times the mills were often closed, with serious consequences for the owners, but with even more devastating consequences for the employees. During good times the company extended credit in their stores as a convenience. In bad times they had to extend this credit further or risk losing their village families. Debts were sometimes forgiven in order to retain the families whose services the mill could not do without.

In some mill villages, owners opened their own banks. In an era of minimal banking regulations and few safeguards for depositors, workers sometimes became unwitting participants in the speculation and schemes of the owners. There was plenty of opportunity for wrongdoing since the mill owners controlled credit and all flow of money. Taking the company storekeepers to task, Hannah Borden of Fall River was able to prove a pattern of overcharges on her store account. She demanded to be paid in cash, not credit, and she got her way, but only after promising to tell no one else in the mill.[9]

The panics of 1829 and 1837 revealed the vulnerability of the workers in the mill village environment. When better times returned, what little bond that had existed between the owners and workers was gone. The workers did not share in the potential profits of expansion and speculation, nor did they appreciate suffering the consequences of management mistakes and miscalculations.

There were many success stories, but many failures as well. In Fall River, Jedediah Tracy recalled the start of his mill in 1813: "We were all ignorant of our undertaking, but had very great expectations from what we had been told." The crises of 1829 and 1837 hurt many people and illustrated that much of the cotton fever investment had been highly speculative. As Erastus Richardson noted in 1876:

> The factory system was the burden of everyone's speech . . . but the fun of the thing was in the fact that there was no system whatever about it. Farmers, blacksmiths, tanners—Tom, Dick and Harry —had tumbled headlong into it, apparently unconscious that system, skill and knowledge of the business were at all necessary to its successful and profitable development. There were mills, machines, cotton and labor, which, if properly handled, would have produced handsome results. But the effluvia and the architecture of the mills was infernal, and the arrangement of the machinery a matter of the smallest concern.[10]

Inferior, dated equipment was another issue raised in a critical appraisal by James Montgomery, an agent for the York Manufacturing Company, a Boston Associates mill in Saco, Maine, who wrote in 1844: "The whole of the cotton factories throughout this district, from Blackstone to Pawtucket, are of an inferior grade. Much of the machinery is old and dirty, while the work is deficient in both quantity and quality."[11] Only one mill in Woonsocket and one in Lonsdale impressed Montgomery as being "modern."

By 1844, a great many of the mills in the Blackstone valley were twenty or more years old and many had been started with extremely limited resources. Jedediah Tracy of Fall River noted, "Our establishment is very small compared with many of the eastern works' and our buildings and machinery are not after the modern improvements, but we cannot afford to throw them by."[12]

Sometimes the machinery hadn't been so good to begin with. "The looms went so wretched poor," Hannah (Borden) Cook recalled of her work as a weaver in Troy (Fall River) in 1817, "that they were constantly being tinkered. When they became too troublesome Mr. Anthony took them to pieces and carried them to Pawtucket to be changed."[13]

Despite the challenges of limited capital and second-rate machinery, Rhode Island manufacturers were not overwhelmed by their "eastern" competitors, even though leadership in textiles had slipped from Rhode Island to Massachusetts as a result of the Boston Associates and the spread of mills up the Blackstone Valley into Massachusetts and in the Fall River area. The free-for-all environment that characterized development of the Blackstone Valley was disorganized compared to the highly regulated development of northern factory cities. Yet it was in the small villages of southern New England that creativity and inventiveness in cloth production could still be found. The small New England mill villages were still, in aggregate, a force to be reckoned with in the textile industry.

Chapter 7

The Waltham Power Loom: Investing in Power Weaving

By 1813, there were some twenty-four hundred power looms in England, but none yet in America. The weaving of cloth in America by power equipment was long overdue. In New England, hand weaving was still the only way to turn machine-spun yarns into cloth. Greater efficiency and productivity could be achieved if home weavers were replaced by factory machines. But this investor's dream posed technological and organizational challenges that would require an unprecedented commitment of capital.

Only the Boston Associates, a closely held association of wealthy merchants and financiers, could afford the investment and eventually made a small fortune in power weaving in Waltham, Massachusetts. As Zachariah Allen noted in 1861, in hindsight: "This manufacturing enterprise (at Waltham) appears to have been the earliest attempt made in the United States with ample funds. . . ."[1]

Earlier, in the late 1780s, Moses Brown and other Providence merchants had diverted money from commerce to manufacturing in Pawtucket. Now, nearly twenty-five years later, this new group of merchants, the Boston Associates, stood prepared to risk their money in cotton manufacturing and do so at an unprecedented level. Their agenda called for the construction of new mills along the Charles River in Waltham near their own turf in Boston, as well as the construction of new machinery, particularly power looms. Backed by a commitment of $100,000, the Boston Manufacturing Company was incorporated in 1813, a mill building was erected and work was underway on a mechanized loom by 1814. Their experiments in power weaving machinery created the industrial city of Waltham and a whole new system of New England textile factories.

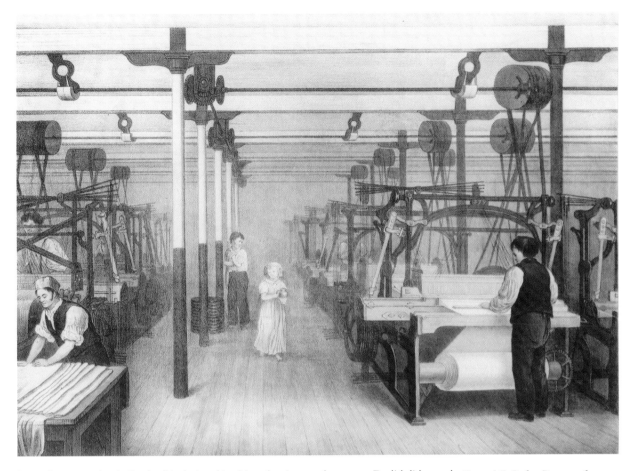

Power loom weaving in England is depicted in this early-nineteenth-century English lithograph. *(Source: J. R. Barfoot,* Progress of Cotton. *Courtesy Slater Mill Historic Site.)*

The Boston Manufacturing Company's famous mills in Waltham, Massachusetts, were depicted in this oil painting by Elijah Smith, ca. 1826–1839. This detail from the painting shows Mill No. 1 (1814–1816) with cupola, Mill No. 2 (1815–1819), and a small machine shop. These brick mills were prototypes for numerous mills built by those seeking to emulate Waltham's success. The first power looms were successfully used in these mills, where finished cloth was produced from raw fibers, and all the steps took place under one roof. *(Courtesy Gore Place.)*

The Integrated Factory

The mechanized loom integrated all aspects of cloth manufacture, from raw fiber to finished fabric, in one sequential process. At the same time, the Boston Manufacturing Company created the first integrated cotton factory in America, a factory in which all the processes—from unpacking cotton bales to packing finished cloth—were managed under one roof. Maximum management control could be exercised in an integrated mill which no longer needed to rely on the "put-out" system of sending out work. This appealed to the Boston Associates, whose aim was to lower manufacturing costs and raise profits. They would build the mills with their pooled wealth and institute a new professional level of business management.

An important element in achieving the integrated factory was to narrow the scope of the mill's work. Each mill would specialize in one product suited to the capacity of the available machinery. Sheeting, the sole product in Waltham, for example, was in constant production, available only in one weight and one color (bleached white). The first yard was identical to the last. The Boston Associates gambled that the efficiency of producing only one coarse grade of cotton cloth would outweigh the lack of product diversity. They would make what their power looms were best suited to make—and that would be sufficient. Though they would fill a relatively small part of the cloth market, they could dominate and control it. This became the goal for the integrated factory.

Experimenting with the Power Loom in America

The Boston Associates did not actually build the first or even the best power loom of the era, but their loom was an outstanding commercial success. Reproducing the complex motions of weaving required precision, timing, and the coordination of many separate actions, including the throwing of the shuttle, the movement of the batten, and the speed of the take-up roll.

As with the spinning machine, cloning the loom was a formidable task. The Boston Associates hired many of the region's best mechanics to develop, design, and build machinery. Betting on expanding investment in textile manufacturing by themselves and others, they authorized construction of a brick machine shop in 1816. The shop's mechanics supported the needs of the mills at Waltham and also built machinery for sale to others. For the Boston Associates, the principal mechanical assistance came from Paul Moody who had worked as a weaver of woolens with the Scolfield brothers in Newburyport. In Moody the Boston Associates found an indispensable ally, a skilled mechanic who played a major role in building the loom and who would later manage the Waltham machine shop.

By patenting their innovations, the Boston Associates also profited from the licensing of their rights. In 1821, for instance, the company leased the rights to all of its patents to the Dover Cotton Factory for a period of five years for a sum of $6,000. In addition to making cloth, the Boston Associates became factory developers, a role they would later expand dramatically in the development of the city of Lowell.

Lacking the enormous capital of the Boston entrepreneurs, the Rhode Island mills were slower to invest in new technology, though they had started experimenting with weaving machinery earlier. Experiments there did not lead to a successful power loom until 1817. During the period from 1813 to 1817, power looms of various designs were built by Hines, Arnold, and Company, Job Manchester, John Thorpe, Elisha Ingraham, Silas Sheperd of Taunton, T. A. Williams—and finally, William Gilmore and David Wilkinson.

William Gilmore, who arrived in Rhode Island in 1815, designed Rhode Island's first successful power loom, the finest loom built in America at that time. Gilmore's "scotch" or "crank" loom soon became the standard in American mills. It was simple, easier to run, and less costly than those used in Waltham. Receiving encouragement from the Lyman Cotton Manufacturing Company in Pawtucket, Gilmore constructed his first loom in 1816. David Wilkinson, one of the great mechanics of the age, was brought in for consultation. (He rendered

This daguerreotype dating from about 1850 is believed to be the oldest surviving American image of a weaver using a power loom. *(Courtesy American Textile History Museum.)*

Gilmore's loom operational by 1817.) After Wilkinson purchased Gilmore's patent for ten dollars, he built his own crank looms, which he sold within weeks. At the same time, similar looms were built at the Dover Cotton Factory.

The first power looms were limited in what they could produce. Hand looms were still required for the production of finer cloth and color changes to form weave patterns, giving the smaller mills of Rhode Island the opportunity to produce more diverse products. The Boston Manufacturing Company forced their Rhode Island competitors out of some markets, but the need for diversity of cloth still allowed smaller mills good profits and growth collateral. Storekeepers wanted to carry a wide assortment of goods. So in 1821, when Portland,

Maine, merchants Rogers and Cox advertised "Waltham water loom shirting and sheeting," they also offered "checks and stripes" that were still made on hand looms, certainly not products of Waltham.

In Webster, Samuel Slater resisted the use of power looms until 1825, preferring the higher-quality work that could be produced on hand looms. As late as 1826, only one-third of Rhode Island mills were using power looms. As late as 1832, a full 10 percent of the state's mills produced only yarn. The putting-out system was sustained by many Rhode Island mills in the face of the development of Waltham and Lowell. Rather than compete directly with these big manufacturers, Rhode island mills concentrated on producing higher-quality goods with superior filling yarn spun on the mule.

A banknote produced for the Sanford (Maine) Bank in the 1860s features a stock engraving of a power loom similar to that used on the Merrimack Manufacturing Company's cloth label. Both images depict a loom that was obsolete by the 1840s. *(Courtesy Maine State Museum.)*

As the use of power looms rapidly spread, production of coarse plain shirting and sheeting increased dramatically, precipitating a decline in the cost of cotton cloth. Waltham sheeting declined from thirty cents a yard in 1816 to only thirteen cents a decade later. This drop in price became characteristic of virtually all textile manufacturing in New England. Increased productivity would make cloth increasingly abundant, affordable, and available. The inexorable march from eighteenth-century sparse wardrobes to twentieth-century walk-in closets had begun.

A cloth label used on merchandise produced by the Merrimack Manufacturing Company, Lowell's first textile corporation. Note the power loom and the calico printing machine, two important new types of machinery, featured on the label. *(Courtesy American Textile History Museum.)*

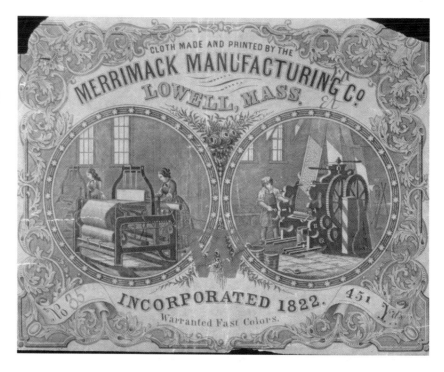

Cloning Waltham

With its focused efficiency, the Boston Manufacturing Company was a phenomenal success. The company set a standard for textile mill profits during its first decade. Its dividends averaged nearly 19 percent per year, a standard never again matched. The extraordinary profits of Waltham lured more entrepreneurs into the business. Manufacturers and merchants attempted to reproduce the Waltham formula for themselves in several northern New England locations.

The best sites offered the required waterpower and were located with convenient access to water routes and the Boston market. The Piscataqua River drainage leading to the port of Portsmouth, New Hampshire, for example, was nearly ideal. Here, since the seventeenth century, the confluence of water power and access to the sea had fostered the development of sawmills and shipyards. Upstream from Portsmouth were Great Bay and smaller bays fed by river drainages. The Salmon River between New Hampshire and Maine, the Cocheco in Dover, New Hampshire, and the Lamprey in Newmarket drew investors from Portsmouth and from Salem, Massachusetts, as well as capitalists from Boston. All sought to clone the success of Waltham.

Dover earned the distinction of being the first factory city patterned directly on the Waltham model. The Dover Cotton Factory was built in 1813 by Portsmouth and Dover merchants. After signing the contract for patent rights, the company built a new mill on the Cocheco River. Following the Waltham lead, they also built a machine shop. Having bought the use of the patents, they hoped to make their own copies of Waltham machinery.

Between the building of the Waltham mills, starting in 1814, and the development of the more sophisticated Lowell mills, beginning in 1821, there were a number of factory developments based on the Waltham model launched by entrepreneurs in several communities. But the money trail led inevitably back to Boston. With few exceptions, the new "Walthams" sooner or later hit hard times and were reorganized and absorbed by the same group of Boston insiders. Though factories and mill villages could be easily started by outsiders, the wealth of the Boston Associates was necessary for survival.

The "weave shed" at the Talbot Mill in Billerica, Massachusetts, ca. 1875. *(Courtesy American Textile History Museum.)*

The "weave shed" at the Continental Mill, in Lewiston, Maine, ca. 1875. *(Courtesy Maine Historic Preservation Commission.)*

One of the few independent companies that held out was the Newmarket Manufacturing Company, which erected three Waltham-type cotton factories between 1822 and 1827 with money from Salem.

The two mills built at Waltham by the Boston Associates served as incubators for the business strategies that would define the spread of textile factories based on the "Waltham system." As compared to most "Rhode Island system" mills, those following the Waltham model were generally larger, were capitalized at a higher level by corporations, and were built on larger waterpower sites and powered through a series of canals.

According to this model it was important to contain labor costs, yet the complexity of power loom weaving required more care and attention than could be expected from a labor force of children. For its labor, the Waltham system relied mostly on young single women. Boardinghouses were built to provide for these "girls." This became a principle characteristic of cities built on the Waltham model. The potential for further development using the Waltham corporation model seemed boundless, but it was in fact limited by the modest waterpower available on the Charles River.

Chapter 8

"The Best Wheel in the World": Waterpower in New England

In September 1823, the agent for the Merrimack Manufacturing Company, Kirk Boott, met at the site of the company's new mill in Lowell with mechanic Paul Moody and principal shareholder Nathan Appleton. They had come to see the progress on the factory and, particularly, its water-wheels. One of the two large breast wheels was in motion. At thirty feet in diameter and twelve feet wide, it was larger than any wheel yet built in Rhode Island. They found the wheel "moving round his course, majestically and with comparative silence."[1] Appleton spent an hour watching it that day and Moody declared it to be "the best wheel in the world." This was good news to the men designing what would become the factory city of Lowell. Its success would be defined, in part, by the excellence of its waterpower engineering.

In eighteenth-century New England there was no clear distinction between mill and machine. Each mill was a single-purpose machine, integrating power, mill structure, and machinery. The water-wheel was built with the mill and was not considered separate. This wheel, the building, and the working components were all part of the same entity. Thus, if one needed the action of a trip hammer, the flow of water would be started, the wheel would turn, and then the hammer would start. Often, each operation had its own wheel, controlled by its own water gate. The operators of an anchor forge in eighteenth-century Pawtucket remembered that "there was a hammer wheel which carried two triphammers, one large and one small, but not both at the same time. . . . There was also three bellows wheels . . . and sometimes a grindstone was attached to the hammer wheel."[2]

Such a rudimentary and unreliable system could not meet the needs of a cotton-spinning mill. And not until later development of these mills did the

Gearing at the Wilkinson Mill is used to raise and lower the gate to regulate the flow of water to the waterwheel. *(Photo by Chris Rivard. Courtesy Slater Mill Historic Site.)*

"machine" become truly independent of its building and its wheel. When Samuel Slater operated textile machinery in the rented space of Ezekiel Carpenter's fulling mill, it was recollected, "the Fulling Mill did not go with said machinery, but they were both operated with the same wheel."[3]

The increasing sophistication of textile machinery demanded improvements in water wheels, speed controls and power distribution. The jack-of-all-trades approach of the traditional millwright gave way to an era of increasing specialization and professional engineering. When William Fisher out-

This wooden breast wheel has been reconstructed in the original wheel pit of the 1810 Oziel Wilkinson Mill in Pawtucket, Rhode Island. The reconstruction was guided by an archeological investigation of the wheel pit area in the 1970s and by documentary evidence filed in federal court records. *(Photo by Chris Rivard. Courtesy Slater Mill Historic Site.)*

fitted a new mill in Thompson, Connecticut, in 1829, for example, the wheel was built by specialists in Sturbridge, Massachusetts.

Mechanics of the Power Wheel

If Ezekiel Carpenter's fulling mill in eighteenth-century Pawtucket was built like most others, the hammers were raised by the action of the main shaft of the water wheel. When the wheel moved, the hammers moved. For this mill to run the water frames and jennies being assembled there by Moses Brown, some means was needed to distribute the power to individual machines, allowing each to be started or stopped as needed. This transmission of power was essential for the entire system to work.

Along with Arkwright-type machinery came ideas for powering it. These machines were portable —no longer built into the mill's architecture and not connected directly to the waterwheel. Power

Two sections of square iron shafting, probably dating from the 1820s, have survived at the Wilkinson Mill in Pawtucket. Here, a vertical shaft that once carried a large iron bevel gear has been reused as a window lintel near the wheel pit. Square iron shafting was extremely heavy, poorly balanced, and slow moving. *(Photo by Chris Rivard.)*

Until the 1830s, heavy iron shafting and gearing were needed to transmit power throughout the mill from the waterwheel up. The gears shown here transfer the motion of the wheel to the top floors at the Wilkinson Mill. *(Photo by Chris Rivard. Courtesy Slater Mill Historic Site.)*

was conveyed to the machines through a system of shafts, gears, and pulleys. This power-distribution system was a feature of every mechanized textile mill and continued until the age of electricity. At first, the network of "line" shafts was made mostly of wood, using technology common to the making of wagon axles and ship masts and spars.

Oziel Wilkinson's Pawtucket cotton mill was an example of power transmission technology as it existed in 1810. Power was conveyed up from the breast wheel, using a large bevel gear on the wooden shaft of the wheel, connected to another bevel gear on a vertical iron shaft. Bevel gears at each floor transferred power to a long sequence of iron shafts, coupled together and turning on wooden bearings. Both the vertical and horizontal shafts were forged of square iron, eight feet long, turned round only at the bearing points.

The result was heavy and slow. Just getting this massive weight of iron moving throughout the building consumed a lot of power, even before one machine was started. The structural failure of some early mills was attributed to the weight of the shafting. The waterwheel that so impressed Paul Moody and Nathan Appleton in Lowell would need a better system of power transfer. Improved solutions were to be developed by mechanics in both Rhode Island and Lowell. But in the late eighteenth and early nineteenth centuries, this was not the only problem faced in securing waterpower.

A Matter of Power

Efficiency required reliability, and this was not possible if the supply of water was itself not reliable. Despite an abundance of waterpower in New England, the best sites had become congested. Transportation considerations limited the waterpower sites that were ideal, and often as a consequence these sites were crowded with mills. Near the falls in Pawtucket, mills had been built from the late seventeenth century, occupying nearly every square inch of space along the waterways and using up all available power. Throughout New England, mills shared the use of water; deeds to mill sites often specified conditions for their water use. Squabbles were common, and with the steady growth in the number of mills, such inefficiency could not continue. In preparation for operating the newly constructed Slater Mill in 1792, Almy, Brown and Slater built a new dam across the Blackstone River above the previously existing dam and falls. On August 31, 1792, according to Moses Brown, "a considerable part of the dam was cut down,"[4] following contentions with the common-law rights of those downstream.

The Boston Associates no doubt noticed the difficulties emerging with water rights. Beginning in 1817, Pawtucket mill owners embarked on a lawsuit, *Tyler* v. *Wilkinson*, which was not resolved for generations. Eventually, it would provide the landmark U.S. Supreme Court decision governing water rights. Water feeding the Wilkinson and other mills located below passed under the Slater mill and was governed by the gates they had installed. The Almy, Brown and Slater mill had been forced to respect the rights of their neighbors by agreeing to close their gate at any time when their mill was idle and water was not flowing over it. In planning Lowell, the Boston Associates inherited none of the age-old encumbrances found at older sites. They bought all the adjacent land and all the waterpower. Ultimately, their efforts to control water would lead to the purchase of rights at the headwaters of both the Merrimack River at Lake Winnipesaukee and Squam Lake in the White Mountains.

Most smaller mills built under the Rhode Island system enjoyed no such grand scheme of waterpower, but wrestled to secure reliable power. A description of the use of waterpower in Woonsocket reveals the congestion and inefficiency of unplanned development characteristic of many of the more congested sites along the Blackstone and other New England river sites:

> The total fall of the Blackstone, from the brow of the upper dam to the Bernon wheel apron, is about thirty-one feet—giving say 2,000 horsepower; 14-32 of the river passes into the Bernon pond, and from thence through the wheels of the Bernon mills. Of these fourteen parts, eight parts

This photo of the serious damage done to a mill in Middlefield, New York, provides a rare view of a wooden waterwheel in its typical location within the mill structure. *(Courtesy Robert M. Vogel.)*

Damages to the Ashworth and Jones Mill in Worcester, Massachusetts, ca. 1870s. Shown here is a breast-type wheel, which was undoubtedly covered by a shed extension from the mill. *(Courtesy American Textile History Museum.)*

pass through the wheels of the Globe mills, on the Smithfield side of the river; and the remaining six parts through the wheels of the Ballou, Harris No. 1, the Lyman and the grist mills, on the Cumberland side of the river; 16-32 of the river passes through the wheels of the Lippitt and Harris mills and of the Woonsocket Machine Works, and from thence through the wheels of the Groton and Clinton mills. The remaining 2-32 of the river passes—First through the wheels of the Bartlett Mill, second through the D.N. Paine, now the Lippitt Privelege; and third through the wheels of Pond's warp mill.[5]

In smaller mills, it was necessary to disconnect some machinery to have enough power to run the remainder at a proper speed. When William Fisher was hired in 1820 to run the Killingly, Connecticut, cotton mill, for example, he complained immedi-

ately to David Wilkinson, an owner, to replace "the old-fashioned cotton picker situated in the garret," because it "took as much power to operate it as all the other machinery. Besides it had a very bad effect on the speed of the mill."

The size of these mills was limited by several constraints, some natural, arising from the building technology of the period. Seldom could a mill be more than thirty-five to forty feet wide. A row of posts down the center left a beam span of seventeen to twenty feet, about the maximum expected. The width of roof trusses imposed a similar limitation. As for so many grist and sawmill and other users of waterpower, the waterwheels were frequently inefficient. Consequently, the generated horsepower was often barely adequate. During dry seasons, the quantity of water did not allow the running of even a small mill.

Drawing of the Stevens Mill in North Andover, Massachusetts, shows the 17-foot-diameter breast wheel that provides power through a series of pulleys and belts. Heavy iron gearing was later replaced by leather belting. *(Courtesy American Textile History Museum.)*

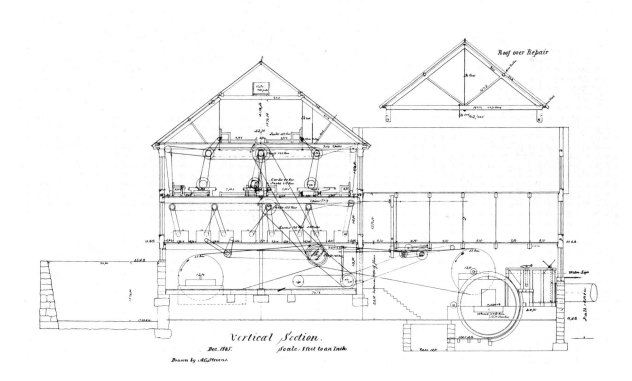

In contrast, the canal system of Lowell was a masterpiece of engineering and it set a model for all large waterpowered city developments to follow. The investors in Lowell were careful about how they used the water, their greatest asset. With canals came an effort to improve on the wooden breast wheel and, at the same time, to find alternatives to the ponderous iron shafting system that wasted power and was blamed for the structural failure of several mills due to its excessive weight. The solution to this power-transfer problem was destined to be a hallmark of American mill construction.

Beginning with the construction of the Appleton Mill in Lowell in 1826, Paul Moody substituted leather belting in place of the heavy, noisy gearing. This was a step in the right direction. In the 1830s, Zachariah Allen at Allendale, Rhode Island, took the belting idea another step by showing that the speed of lightweight shafting and belts could achieve the same power as the slower moving, heavy installations. Higher speed was, in fact, dependent on lighter weight. Improvements in metalworking and the use of cold-rolled shafts and lathes made these technical advances possible. The older shafting plans were replaced by lighter, faster-moving shafting connected to the machinery with belting. The savings of power were enormous; but now, of course, faster machines were demanding faster waterwheels.

The iron water turbine, a much improved use of waterpower first developed in France in 1832, was the logical next step in powering textile mills. Not surprisingly, the principal engineers of Lowell's water system took the lead in improving turbine technology. Chief engineer James Francis and his assistant Uriah A. Boyden developed improved turbines in the 1840s.

By 1850, a new strategy for waterpower was being used in all new mills and retrofitted to most older ones. The design featured a high-efficiency, fast-moving turbine to run a relatively lightweight network of shafts and pulleys connected to one another and to the machinery itself by leather belting. Even the pulleys themselves were made increasingly lightweight. The serpentine spoke pattern used on such pulleys was useful in keeping the thin spokes from cracking as the castings cooled. The waterwheels of Pawtucket and Lowell had come a long, long way.

Chapter 9

Genius, Wealth, and Industry: Lowell Astonishes the World

When the Boston Associates dispatched their representatives to scout the land around Pawtucket Falls in Chelmsford, Massachusetts, they were discrete. Soon they would negotiate to purchase the existing Pawtucket Canal, the waterpower on this stretch of the Merrimack and the land within a sharp bend in the river. Here, in 1821, the representatives—two of Francis Cabot Lowell's relatives, Nathan Appleton and Patrick Tracy Jackson—envisioned a cotton-manufacturing city more ambitious that anything yet imagined, a city that would astonish America and much of the world.

The bold scheme to create the city of Lowell grew from an idea hatched by Francis Cabot Lowell around 1810. Rejecting advice from his uncle George Cabot (who had lost money in an unsuccessful attempt to spin cotton in Beverly, Massachusetts), Lowell prepared to invest in manufacturing cotton. In England, Lowell visited cotton mills and studied their machinery, paying special attention to some recently developed power looms. The Boston Associates would eventually sponsor his research, which would lead to the power mills of Lowell.

When the Boston Associates had outgrown their limited waterpower site on the Charles River in Waltham, the search began for a site that might provide power for the next stage of their factory expansion. The plan culminated in the city of Lowell, named for the Associates' leader and founder, John Cabot Lowell, who had died in 1817.

The development plan was encouraged by the purchase of several properties near the falls that could be modified for power to the mills. The Pawtucket Canal had been built to allow passage of barges around the falls and rapids in 1792. Now this waterway could be converted to a flume delivering water to a number of mill sites. A second man-made

Lowell presented a stunning new cityscape in America, as depicted in this 1834 lithograph. In the 1830s, Lowell was still growing, but this scene from Dracut was already very impressive. *(Courtesy American Textile History Museum.)*

Mills built by Boston financiers followed the plan first established in Waltham. This version, built in Methuen in the 1820s, is the last surviving example of this architectural style in Massachusetts. *(Courtesy American Textile History Museum.)*

The York Manufacturing Company was established in Saco, Maine, in 1829. Here, Boston investors found a nearly perfect site for a Lowell-style development. The power of the Saco River came down to the sea and vessels could easily approach the mill sites. *(Source: James Montgomery,* A Practical Detail of the Cotton Manufacture of the United States of America, *1840. Courtesy American Textile History Museum.)*

improvement, the Middlesex Canal, provided access to the Boston market. Completed in 1804, this twenty-seven-mile water route from Chelmsford to Boston was ideal for the delivery of raw materials and groceries, and the transport of manufactured products to their market.

Moving quickly, representatives of the Boston investors bought the water rights, the Pawtucket Canal, and adjacent land for a bargain price of $70,000 before local farmers and landowners fully realized what was happening. With construction beginning in 1822, this city would enjoy an unbelievable decade of continuous growth that would make it the country's premier industrial city.

Development Mission for a City

The Boston merchants embarked on their bold plan for tapping the Merrimack River's power at

The Brunswick Company Mill in Brunswick, Maine, as illustrated on a stock certificate, 1840. *(Courtesy American Textile History Museum.)*

The Belknap Mill, built in 1823 in Laconia, New Hampshire, is among the last surviving factory structures exhibiting the common characteristics of mills in the style of Waltham and Lowell. *(Photo by Chris Rivard.)*

The Buziel Mill in Laconia, New Hampshire, follows the architectural design of its earlier neighbor, the Belknap Mill. *(Photo by Chris Rivard.)*

Chelmsford. Draining a watershed of over four thousand square miles, the potential power of the river was enormous. Even a small wing dam using only a part of the power was capable of running some fifty cotton mills.

The potential of the Merrimack River in Chelmsford was much greater than the Associates needed. The original Boston Associates could not, themselves, use all the waterpower. To justify such an investment, many mills would need to be built and for that purpose the investor circle was enlarged into a corporation, calling itself the Merrimack Manufacturing Company. In addition to producing cloth, the Merrimack Manufacturing Company's development mission was to create the canal system, design and build the mills using this power, and construct the machinery needed to outfit the mills. An entire new area of investment and profit arose from their activities. To manage this new business,

the old "Proprietors of the Locks and Canals Company" that had built the Pawtucket Canal was resurrected as a subsidiary corporation. Substantial profits awaited the leasing of water rights and the building of mills and machinery. Under the leadership of this new development company, the city began its extraordinary growth with the construction of seventeen mills within the next five years. The income generated from leases alone yielded a half million dollars a year.

Lowell was a city planned by hydraulic engineers. The extension of canals was destined to continue through building campaigns from 1822 to 1848. Along the canals were mill sites and cotton mills. Borrowing a strategy pioneered in the housing of workers at the Great Falls Manufacturing Company in Great Falls, New Hampshire, boardinghouses were built adjacent to the mill structures. In Lowell, the needs of manufacturing came first.

Sample of gingham cloth produced by the Lancaster Mill in Clinton, Massachusetts, in 1848. Initially rejected by cotton manufacturers in Lowell, the Crompton loom demonstrated its capacity to produce patterned cloth in woolen mills. Using this same technology, cotton mills began production of "scotch" plaids, gingham, and figured cloth known as "nankeens." *(Courtesy American Textile History Museum.)*

Sample of gingham produced by the Lancaster Mill in Clinton, Massachusetts, 1848. *(Courtesy American Textile History Museum.)*

Then attention was paid to organizing the factory workforce and its needs.

Creating a Workers' Environment

During its first decade, the city of Lowell was a marvel. Boston's commercial families invested their wealth to support the new ideas and mechanical genius that created this aspiring industrial city. Lowell grew dramatically by replicating the mills first built at Waltham and creating an industrial landscape never before seen in America. The city of Lowell came to symbolize all that was good about the new industrial order—as well as all that was bad.

At first, Lowell seemed to prove that factories could uplift the lives of people—in particular, the women workers. Visitors to Lowell, from President Andrew Jackson to Charles Dickens, were struck by the promise of the city, marveling at its capacity to make cloth and at the same time achieve decent living conditions for workers. The *Essex Gazette* echoed the sentiments of many when it noted: "It is indeed a fairy scene. Here we beheld an extensive city, busy, noisy, and thriving, with immense prospects of increasing extent and boundless wealth. Everything is fresh and green with the vigor of youth. . . . What cannot a combination of genius wealth and industry produce!"[1] Michael Chevalier, writing for a French audience in 1836, noted: "Lowell is not amusing, but it is neat and decent, peaceful and sage."[2]

Following the plan used in Waltham, the mills in Lowell solicited the work of young women who lived in factory-run boardinghouses during their temporary labor in the mills. In order to entice these young women to move to Lowell, the housing had to be decent and secure. Owners imposed a strict code of conduct and curfews to create what they considered a high moral climate for the community. It was more likely the prevailing sensibilities of the young women themselves, and indeed of the whole culture, however, that did most to maintain discipline. While most visitors were struck by the audacious size of the building program, they were also awed by the spectacle of a city filled with attractive, well-dressed young women.

The story of the "mill girls" has often dominated the story of Lowell itself. Women were an integral part of the story of the city. In its first decade, conditions seemed almost utopian compared to life on New England farms. Cash wages were paid, which meant that young women, for the first time, could escape from the total financial control of male heads of households. As the word of Lowell spread, recruitment was not a problem. The hours of work were long by modern standards, but better than the never-ending farm work.

The mill girls did much to generate the cachet of Lowell. When some of the "girls" started their own literary publication, *The Lowell Offering*, it seemed to provide evidence of the social benefits of the factory working environment. For those who argued that factories could bring with them an uplifting social order, Lowell was living proof.

Though the development of Lowell redefined the potential of textile investment in America, the Boston Associates could not monopolize production, despite their commercial power, for very long. Competition was inevitable, and there were other issues. Other aspiring entrepreneurs soon copied the system of raising capital by forming corporations. The Boston investors, by leasing waterpower sites and building machinery, themselves sowed the seeds of overcapacity to produce. Their growth was driven by the potential for profit, not by the laws of supply and demand. Their concept of the integrated factory was neither dynamic nor flexible. Overcapacity to produce coarse, plain goods was inevitable, and the stampede toward profit would one day lead to hardship and losses. The glory days of Lowell were destined to pass.

Chapter 10

Calico, Blocks, and Rollers: Printing Technology and the New Fashion

A new class of imported cotton goods landed on American wharves at the end of the War of 1812. These goods were not coarse and certainly not plain. In fact, there were now a great variety of choices, including cotton goods sporting a wide assortment of colorful printed designs—mostly made by machine. New England's manufacturers faced another technological challenge. Printing technology would provide the product diversity that had been missing in the products of the region's large integrated cotton factories.

By midcentury, the Merrimack Manufacturing Company placed labels on all their bolts of cloth. This company logo displayed a power loom along with a roller printing press, which had become equally important in producing the company's products. While power looms had woven their many miles of "grey goods," roller printing machines had transformed this cloth into colorful fabrics. The new technology provided a major improvement to the plain cloth previously produced in Waltham. It answered the need for variety and fashion consciousness without requiring a change in the system of efficient fiber-to-cloth production used by the larger integrated factories of New England. When the Boston Associates launched Lowell's first cotton mill, the Merrimack Manufacturing Company, in 1822, they envisioned not just another factory to produce plain cloth, but a bleachery and calico-printing plant to turn their "grey goods" into a variety of printed designs that would accommodate home furnishings, shirting, and dress goods.

The Printing Process

The printing techniques that had been used in the printing of books and graphic prints for centuries

The concept of printing designs on plain cloth was well understood, but the artistic skills needed to produce wooden printing blocks limited the use of printing as a domestic activity. This linen and cotton bedspread, owned by the Nancy Corbly Clark family in Ohio, ca. 1830, was printed with blocks. *(Courtesy American Textile History Museum.)*

were now adapted for textiles. In England, prints on cotton from India had been a novelty as early as the fifteenth century and had become popular by the mid-seventeenth century. In fact, the name "calico" derived from the principal port of shipment, Calcutta. Despite initial resistance, printed textiles were soon produced in both England and France.

At first, printing was a hand process using hardwood blocks. But printing could also be achieved by engraving the design of copper plates. Here the pattern was incised on the plate, the color applied and then wiped from the surface, leaving color only in the incised pattern. By pressing the cloth and the copper plate together, the design was transferred to the cloth. Though engraved prints required craft

skills and were painstaking and expensive, they held the promise of mechanical improvement. If the copper plates were transposed onto the surface of a cylinder, the design could be turned against the cloth continuously. The engraved rollers could be run by waterpower to achieve the level of mass production that appealed to mill operators.

Creating roller printing machines was only the latest challenge for New England machine builders, who were already adept at cloning machinery. But this new technology required experienced machine operators. Because the demands of printing were part science and part art, the roller printing machine involved a variety of indispensable skills. Artists were needed to create designs and—even when de-

When the Springvale Print Works was incorporated in 1828, investors built a factory space for its blocking tables and printing machines near a spring along the Mousam River. Three houses for workers were also built along the "brow of the hill," as well as the company store seen in the foreground. *(Courtesy Sanford Historical Committee.)*

signs were pirated from others (the rule more than the exception)—someone had to draw the designs, isolate elements to be added by each roller, and engrave them. Even the scientific mixing of colors was complex. For example, not all colors could be permanently "fixed" into the cloth. Madder, a common chemical choice producing pink and brown colors, was not accepted by cloth unless it was treated with an intermediate chemical called a "mordant."

Competition in Printing

Though the first efforts to print cloth were in Philadelphia, it was in New England that a high industrial level of production was achieved. In the 1820s, the three New England firms at the forefront of printing production were in Dover, New Hamp-

shire; Taunton, Massachusetts; and Lowell. Espionage was rife among them, and the pirating of employees unrelenting. As the fickle fortunes of fashion continually changed, printing presented many design opportunities. While mills had produced standardized goods for decades, most print designs lasted only for one fashion season. Thus the need for artists, designers, engravers, and colorists was continuous.

Turning "grey goods" into many thousands of print designs also required experienced managers to run the print works. It was clear that experienced workers and managers from England, particularly from the Lancashire district, were required in America. Each of the rival start-up companies sent their representatives to England in search of experienced experts and machinery information. Experienced printers knew the value of their services. Luring

Two men with printing blocks, ca. 1870. Printing with carved wooden blocks survived well into the age of roller printing machinery. Finished consumer items, such as shawls, sometimes required the block printing of a border on all four sides. Later, block printing survived in the manufacture of oilcloth and linoleum floor coverings. *(Courtesy American Textile History Museum.)*

With the use of engraved rollers the printing process became more efficient and fast. Suddenly, inexpensive cotton prints flooded the market with a great variety of fashion choices. *(Source: J. A. Barfoot, lithograph,* The Progress of Cotton. *Courtesy Slater Mill Historic Site.)*

Aaron Peasley away from the Merrimack Manufacturing Company, an agent at Dover wrote, in 1825: "If we obtain a man of Mr. Peasley's ingenuity we must purchase him at a dear rate, but what is that to getting two or three years' start in the business?"[1] When attempting to lure John Dynley Prince from Manchester, England, to Lowell, the Merrimack Manufacturing Company was shocked by Prince's demand for a salary of one thousand pounds a year. The Merrimack representative told him the sum was more than the governor of Massachusetts earned in a year. Prince reportedly answered, "But can your Governor print?"[2]

Recruiting skilled workers in England became easier with the relaxation of Britain prohibition on the legal immigration of its mechanics in 1824. Workers and supervisors were allowed to leave England and return home again if they wished. Even with this greater freedom to recruit, the competition was fierce. The Dover company sought an individual in 1826 who was "knowledgeable in the highest classes of work" and was "nothing short of superior to Prince [at Merrimack] or Yates [at Taunton]."[3]

Roller Printing Technology

Once the printing works of Dover, Taunton, and Lowell were running successfully, the use of printing technology grew dramatically, supported by continuing immigration from Europe and by new expertise developed in America. While the mid-1820s saw the pioneer companies struggling, a

Samuel Dunster is believed to have been among the first American-born men to learn and master the calico printer's trade. He moved extensively through the Northeast, working and sometimes investing in calico printing works. This page from a Dunster sample book dates from 1832. *(Courtesy Rhode Island Historical Society.)*

decade later New England companies were able to produce a staggering annual production of 120 million yards of cotton prints. As early as 1831–32, three Massachusetts companies at Taunton, Lowell, and Fall River were themselves producing over 20 million yards of calico per year.

Roller printing technology provided the impetus for this remarkable growth. Armed with some patterns and machine parts, New England machinists could build and eventually improve these machines. At the same time, block printing also increased, particularly in the production of items like shawls that required finished print borders on all sides. During the years of experimentation, John Williams of the Dover company noted: "I have no doubt we shall use cylinders soon, must though, begin with blocks."[4] Block cutters and printers were among the trades sought by New England printers.

With the development of bleacheries, dye houses, and printing works, the art of preparing and fixing dyes became even more important and with it the job of "textile colorist" emerged. The cost of dyestuffs was sometimes even greater than the cost of the labor to run the printing machines. In the mid-1850s, for example, the Manchester Print Works employed a staff of some four hundred men and thirty women with a payroll of $180,000. But the cost of the chemicals was close to $375,000.[5]

As always, machine technology led to further technical change. Although the "standard" generic print cloth featured sixty-four threads per inch, the potential for higher quality printing favored the producers of finer counts of yarn. This encouraged the mule-spinning work of Rhode Island mills to support the print works at Fall River. Though the English printers seriously doubted that mills like Merrimack could make satisfactory prints using the coarse products of throstle frames, the American manufacturers surprised them with their success. Printing also favored the finer cotton cloths pro-

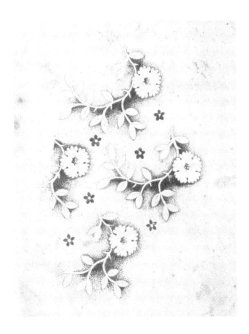

These small watercolor and gouache paintings were produced as designs for calico prints in the early nineteenth century. The artist J. F. Street first established himself as an "Engraver to Calico Printers" in Manchester, England, before he was solicited to come to Dover, New Hampshire, in 1827. *(Courtesy Slater Mill Historic Site.)*

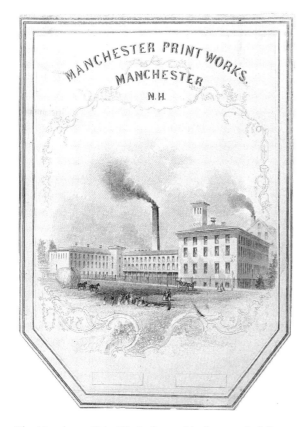

The Manchester Print Works featured its fine new building on its cloth label, produced from 1850 to 1875. *(Courtesy American Textile History Museum.)*

Cloth labels were a form of advertising brand names and guarantees, such as "fast colors." *(Courtesy American Textile History Museum.)*

duced by Rhode Island manufacturers and the products of seacoast mills in Fall River and later New Bedford, where the damp salt air assisted in the spinning of finer counts of yarn.

Seasonal Fashions

Contrary to the concept of regular production in the integrated factory, the production levels of printeries were more seasonal. Although the Manchester Print Works reported an average daily run of thirty-five thousand yards of delaine (cotton warp yarns with worsted filling) and twenty thousand yards of cotton calicos, it was noted at midcentury that this could be increased to eight thousand yards a day during seasons of high demand. Staple products were replaced by fashion-sensitive seasonal products of almost unlimited variety. It was not uncommon for nineteenth-century printing companies to produce more than a thousand new designs each season. Printeries, distributors, and converters were forced to anticipate the fashions or, more often, wait for new fashions to be introduced by

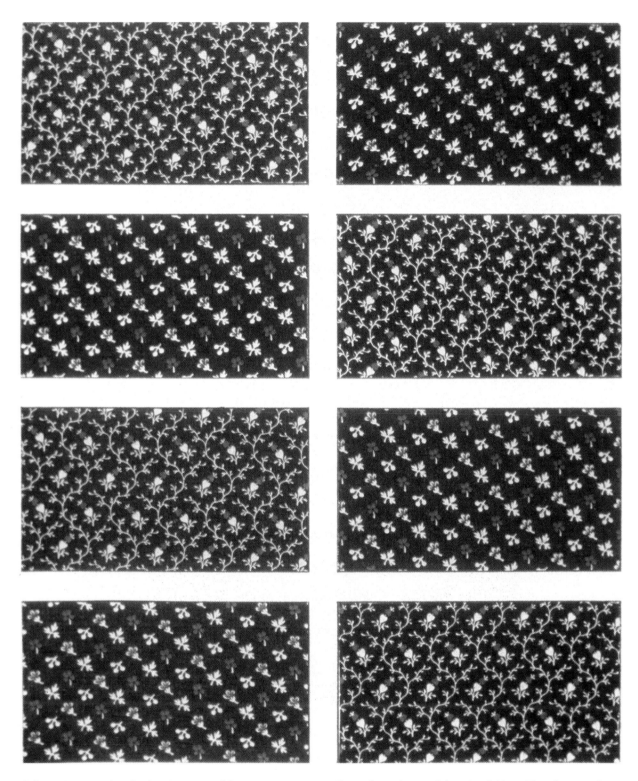

Calico printers produced a dizzying array of designs in an ongoing effort to keep abreast of changing fashions. The selection of Cocheco Print Works samples shown here was offered in 1883. *(Courtesy American Textile History Museum.)*

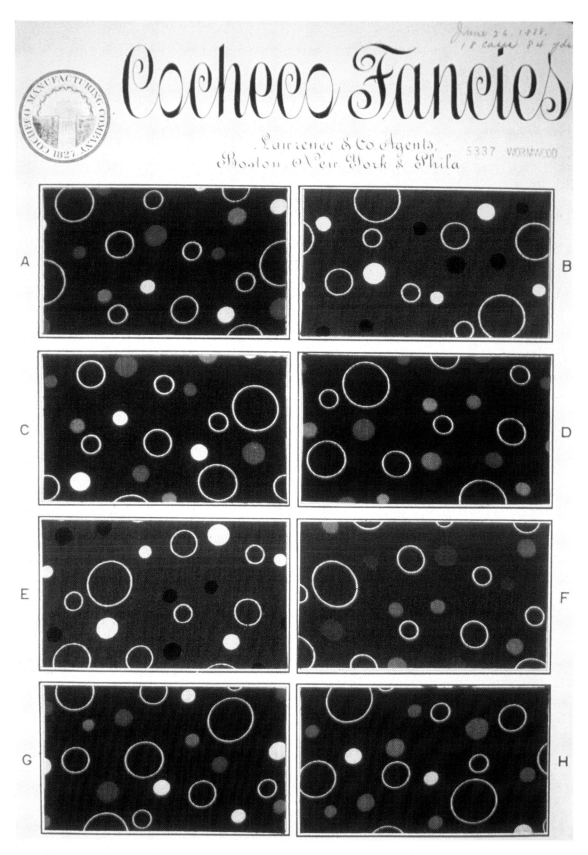

This selection of Cocheco "fancy" prints from 1880 shows a surprisingly modern sense of design. *(Courtesy American Textile History Museum.)*

Ambrotype photo of a man behind the counter of a dry goods store, ca. 1850. An abundance of print cloth was distributed through such retail outlets. Note the woman's dress displayed on a form in the left foreground. *(Courtesy Greg French.)*

European printers—particularly those in France—and then rush to produce similar goods. It was now useless to patent designs, especially in the face of international commerce. Instead, many if not most of the designs appearing in the first American printeries were, in modern parlance, "knock-offs." In a way, it was a revolt against the earlier concept of the integrated factory and its seamless continuity and standardization.

By 1889, America's print cloth production was destined to reach over 800 million yards a year.[6] Some of this cloth was used for home furnishing and

Cotton print dresses, as shown in this detail of a dress from the 1820s, led to greatly expanded women's wardrobes. *(Photo by Chris Rivard. Courtesy American Textile History Museum.)*

underwear but much of it went into the production of women's dresses made in bulk and bought "ready to wear" from the store (rather than from the seamstress). Under the influence of nineteenth-century ready-to-wear clothing, men's fashions became subdued compared to their "peacock" status in the eighteenth century, giving new meaning to the term "grey goods." A democratized generic plainness emerged as the proper business uniform—remaining to this day—while women's clothing took center stage. Enough print cloth was made each year, it was calculated, to make seventeen dresses for every woman in the country. When Americans got around to building closets in their homes, these dresses would quickly fill them up.

Chapter 11

"Simply Preposterous": New England's Woolen Mills Catch Up

When Colonel Francis McLean built a woolen mill in Rockville, Connecticut, in 1821 and proposed that his mill would produce one hundred yards of broadcloth a day, the residents of Rockville considered this "simply preposterous."[1] Few people in America could make broadcloth comparable to the British imports—and certainly not in such large quantities.

By this time woolen cloth had already enjoyed a long history of filling many fundamental family needs. A large variety of basic woolen goods was consistently used for practical items such as shirts, blankets, bedspreads, and underwear. Better woolen goods, on the other hand, were highly prized—gentlemen commonly distinguished themselves through their wardrobes of fine felted broadcloth, for example. Clothing made of broadcloth was often listed among the most valuable items in estate inventories. Most of these finer grades of woolen cloth were imported from England.

Early mills in America rarely attempted to produce fine woolens comparable to British imports. And when these cloths were locally produced, American manufacturers often mimicked the English products, selling them with "fictitious labels, indicating that they [had] a foreign origin."[2] The products of the first documented woolen mill, started in Hartford, Connecticut, in 1788, led Alexander Hamilton to write enthusiastically that the factory had achieved a quality "which surpasses anything that could have been looked for in so short a time and under so great disadvantages."[3] Although New England–made broadcloth was featured in the inaugural outfits of Washington, Jefferson, and Monroe, these manufactures were merely symbolic gestures that expressed hope for the future.

New England woolen manufacturers soon learned the same lesson that cotton manufacturers had

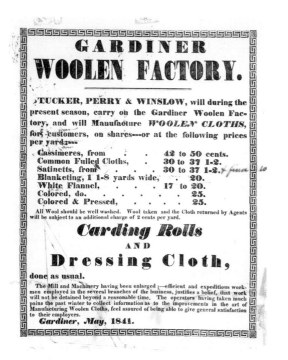

GARDINER
WOOLEN FACTORY.

TUCKER, PERRY & WINSLOW, will during the present season, carry on the Gardiner Woolen Factory, and will Manufacture *WOOLEN CLOTHS*, for customers, on shares---or at the following prices per yard:---

Cassimeres, from . . . . 42 to 50 cents.
Common Fulled Cloths, . . 30 to 37 1-2.
Satinetts, from . . . . 30 to 37 1-2.
Blanketing, 1 1-8 yards wide, . . 20.
White Flannel, ... 17 to 20.
Colored, do. . . . . . 25.
Colored & Pressed, ... 25.

All Wool should be well washed. Wool taken and the Cloth returned by Agents will be subject to an additional charge of 2 cents per yard.

Carding Rolls
AND
Dressing Cloth,

done as usual.

The Mill and Machinery having been enlarged;—efficient and expeditious workmen employed in the several branches of the business, justifies a belief, that work will not be detained beyond a reasonable time. The operators having taken much pains the past winter to collect information as to the improvements in the art of Manufacturing Woolen Cloths, feel assured of being able to give general satisfaction to their employers.
Gardiner, May, 1841.

Many New England woolen mills carried on the traditions of earlier carding and fulling mills by offering a variety of services to local customers. This advertisement from the Gardiner (Maine) Woolen Factory itemized services ranging from carding to custom weaving. *(Courtesy Maine State Museum.)*

Daguerreotype of a man holding a shuttle, ca. 1845. While the workforce of cotton mills was dominated by women, as many as two-thirds of nineteenth-century woolen mill workers were men. *(Courtesy American Textile History Museum.)*

learned: it was impossible to compete with fine British imports. Success in producing woolen goods depended on taking command of the lower-end products. This meant, theoretically, that the work of early woolen mills stood in direct competition with the work of local homes, where as much as two-thirds of New England's woolen cloth was still being made as late as the 1820s. In reality, the mills worked in cooperation with local home industry and continued to provide many individual services to family homes while they inched their way toward true factory status.

A Typical New England Woolen Mill

The experience of Samuel Mayall in Gray, Maine, illustrates a common New England growth pattern. After brief stops in South County, Rhode Island, and on Bunker Hill, Mayall arrived in Gray and started a small-scale carding and cloth finishing mill in 1791. The next step toward the operation of a full-service woolen mill took place in 1804 when he constructed the Gray Woolen Manufactory. Advertising in the *Eastern Argus* in May of 1804, Mayall noted that he was "now ready to receive Sheep's Wool, to break for hatters, to card into Rolls, and to work into various kinds of cloth that may be wanted."[4] Weaving services were offered to produce broadcloth, cottons, blankets, rugs and flannels, "all five-quarters (forty-five inches) wide." Mayall's factory centralized all processes outside the home, but his individual customers usually owned the wool and controlled the products—making them the true manufacturers.

Unlike the Hartford Woolen Manufactory (1788) and the Newburyport Woolen Manufactory (1794), Samuel Mayall did not seek to compete with imported broadcloth. Most New England woolen mills were small and poorly funded. By avoiding "lordly broadcloth," small New England mills cornered the market for lower-grade goods, producing fabrics that had a "common character" and did not require as much skill in production. Beginning with more modest objectives and depending on custom services to the local community, Mayall's mill lasted

This small woolen mill was built in 1842 in East Wilton, Maine. The owners were mostly local farmers with little manufacturing experience and most workers were novices. Girls here were paid $1.50 a week plus board; men received $10 to $15 a month plus board. In 1845, this mill operated two sets of carding machines (six machines) and produced coarse "kerseymeres." The mill was not a success. *(Courtesy Maine Historic Preservation Commission.)*

longer than the factories of his more ambitious contemporaries.

The technology of the first woolen manufacturers did not provide an escape from hand work. While machinery alleviated some of the most burdensome tasks, particularly carding, the pre-1820 woolen mill was often a combination of mechanized and hand operations. Spinning jennies were included in the catalog of machinery in many early mills, but these machines did little to change businesses that, for the moment, were still largely oriented toward local household services. Thus, in

An elegant elevation drawing of the mill in East Wilton, Maine. *(Courtesy Maine Historic Preservation Commission.)*

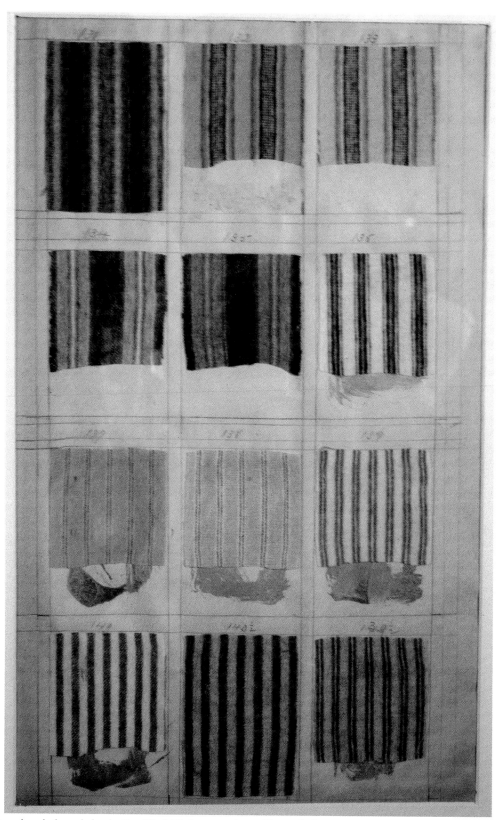

Samples of woolen cloth made by the Franklin Mill show a variety of fancy cloths produced by Crompton-type power looms, ca. late 1860s. *(Courtesy American Textile History Museum.)*

Incorporated in 1830, the Middlesex Woolen Manufacturing Company was the largest woolen establishment in America. Under the leadership of the mill's agent Samuel Lawrence, Middlesex led the way toward the use of the Crompton fancy loom. *(Courtesy American Textile History Museum.)*

1834, Mayall's second mill (now being operated by the company of Thomas and Wilson) advertised that it was "prepared to manufacture common fulled cloth from raw material at 35 cts. per yard, all other woolen cloth in proportion."[5]

Although increasingly archaic in technology and management, custom manufacture of woolens and service to local families continued well into the mid-nineteenth century. Small rural mills and independent weavers participated in an evolving economy partly rooted in the past traditions of domestic work and partly tied to the industrial future. From the 1820s to the 1840s, these relationships included many different configurations. A succession of hand weavers, for example, conducted business in Gorham, Maine, where they specialized in the custom weaving of woolen carpets into the 1850s.

Producing Other Wool-Based Fabrics

At some point, despite the well-established competition from Europe, the prestige and high value of broadcloth enticed the region's largest woolen mills

to meet this challenge head-on. Thus, companies including Samuel Slater and Sons in Webster, Massachusetts, and the Middlesex Woolen Mill in Lowell were producers of broadcloth by 1830. But there were a number of less demanding goods that were popular from the 1810s through the 1840s. These included flannel, cassimere, and satinet—a new product developed in America. Though many of these less expensive cloths were produced in homes, one by one they fell within the orb of the mill.

Flannel was the most basic of all woolen products. Every woolen cloth is technically a "flannel" at one point in its manufacture. The raw product of the loom is flannel. Even broadcloth is flannel before it undergoes the skilled, labor-intensive work of fulling, napping, and shearing. The job of making flannel is relatively simple and the choice always exists to leave the woolen cloth just as it comes from the loom. Used for underwear and work shirts, flannel was not intended for finer clothing and was therefore unaffected by changes in fashion, and so it was logically the first and easiest product for small factories.

Among the earliest pioneer flannel manufacturers

A shortage of skilled clothiers encouraged American manufacturers to mechanize the processes of napping and shearing. This 1930s "vibrating" shearing machine, a technological dead end, was made by Parks and Davidson in Vermont and used at a fulling mill in Alna, Maine. *(Courtesy Maine State Museum.)*

was Abraham Marland of Andover, Massachusetts, and Nathaniel Stevens of nearby North Andover. In 1814, Stevens turned the entire activities of his mill to flannels with notable success. Nathaniel Stevens showed that a significant profit could be made from the mass production of a low-end product. He successfully concentrated on generic flannels from 1814 until his death in 1876. It was, no doubt, to the success of Stevens and Marland that John L. Hayes referred in 1868, when he wrote that "the little mills of Andover and North Andover have wrought out fortunes for their owners in the patient industry for many a year."[6]

Another early flannel producer, the Amesbury (Massachusetts) Flannel Manufacturing Company, was incorporated in 1822 with a capital investment of $200,000 and produced some fifteen hundred pieces of flannel each year. Thanks to these pioneering efforts, by 1824 as much as 690,000 yards of flannel were reportedly made within only forty miles of Boston. Benefitting from the favorable provisions of the Tariff Act of 1828, flannels in solid colors of red, blue, and purple, as well as shirting material in gray and blue, were abundantly produced in New England mills. Mills such as those of

The Sutton Woolen Mill, North Andover, Massachusetts, about 1850. *(Courtesy American Textile History Museum.)*

The Stevens Mill in North Andover, Massachusetts, is seen here in a mid-nineteenth-century oil painting. *(Courtesy American Textile History Museum.)*

the Gonic (New Hampshire) Manufacturing Company and Stirling Mills in Lowell produced flannel by the mile toward the end of the century.

The uses for flannel increased to include linings for overcoats, shirts for workmen, fatigue uniforms for soldiers, and coats for light summer use. Meanwhile, the rapid spread of knitting machine technology after 1850 helped produce knitted goods that replaced many woven flannels for items such as underwear.

A cribbage match at the Stevens Woolen Mill, North Andover, Massachusetts, was captured in this photograph from the 1870s. *(Courtesy American Textile History Museum.)*

Originally built as the Haverhill Flannel Factory, this view of the Stevens Mill in Haverhill, Massachusetts, was painted in 1855. *(Courtesy American Textile History Museum.)*

Use of both cotton and woolen yarn in the production of "mixed" cloth did not appeal to the traditional interests of England. However, in America, the long, strong fibers of flax had been used by home industry in combination with woolen filling yarns for decades to produce coverlets known as "linsey-woolseys." As the growing abundance of machine-spun cotton replaced the use of linen, substituting cotton for linen warps created a new product called "satinet." This was an inadvertent Ameri-

This scene around the Hillsboro Woolen Mill, at Hillsboro Bridge, New Hampshire, was captured in the 1850s. *(Courtesy American Textile History Museum.)*

can "invention." First appearing in New England as early as 1788, satinet was produced in Canton, Massachusetts, in 1808 and by Delano Abbott of Rockville, Connecticut, and Abraham Marland of Andover around 1812. It is likely that the switch from linen to cotton took place independently in many mills and workshops, with each mill believing it was responsible for introducing this new fabric.

Mills took the lead in the manufacture of satinet around 1810, sometimes spinning both the cotton and woolen yarns in one establishment. Satinet was ideally suited to early woolen mills because its manufacture required less skill than broadcloth. In the late 1810s, many called themselves "cotton and woolen" mills. One of the first such companies was the Amesbury Wool and Cotton Company which, starting in 1812, was credited with making satinet the "principal business of the village." Satinet also became the main manufacture for the village of Rockville, Connecticut.

At first, both flannel and satinet were woven by hand. But power looms developed to weave cotton required only slight modifications to weave satinet. Not surprisingly, machine builders like David Wilkinson of Pawtucket quickly saw the market opportunities emerging, and satinet looms were soon being produced along with the line of cotton machinery. Encouraged by power loom weaving, satinet mills sprang up quickly. So great was the success of these mills that, by the 1830s, satinet production constituted nearly one-half of the entire woolen production of America.[7]

Investment in woolen mills lagged significantly behind those for cotton. Still, by 1816 Connecticut alone had twenty-five woolen factories capable of producing a total of 375,000 yards of narrow-width and 125,000 yards of broadcloth. Substantial investments were led by the large mills: Middlesex Woolen Mill in Lowell; Samuel Slater and Company in Webster, Massachusetts; Pontoosuk in Pittsfield, Massachusetts; and the Great Falls Manufacturing Company in Somersworth, New Hampshire.

Several characteristics of woolen production tended to support and sustain the smaller mills as

This lithograph of the Sawyer Woolen Mills in Dover, New Hampshire, includes worker housing in the foreground. *(Courtesy American Textile History Museum.)*

well. The upcoming emphasis on fashion design demanded close attention to detail, as well as a capacity to make sudden changes in production. These specialized needs did not particularly favor larger mills. Even some very small, remote mills could participate in the regional trade of woolen goods. One mill in Dover, Maine, for example, sent its products overland thirty-five miles by oxcart to Bangor, and from there by water to Philadelphia, where the merchandise would be sold. In the production of woolens, bigger had never necessarily meant better.

Chapter 12

Jenny, Jack, and Billy:
The Woolen
Machinery Family

It was agreed in 1841 that Samuel Cooper would receive $50 for the first year of work, $60 for the second year and $80 for the third. This was not much money, but it is likely that Cooper was very pleased. He had been awarded an old-style apprenticeship "for the purposes of learning the business of Machinist."[1] In an era characterized by a labor pool of wage earners, apprenticeship contracts were becoming increasingly scarce. Cooper knew that he might need to endure some early years of relative poverty, but he also knew he would eventually be admitted to the ranks of one of the fastest-growing and highest-paying trades encouraged by the rise of textile manufacture.

This apprenticeship opportunity was also unusual because the employer was a builder of woolen mill machinery: Gilbert, Gleason and Davis of North Andover, Massachusetts. Cotton mills had led the way in the rise of machine shops. Beginning in the 1790s, the spread of mill villages had sustained a growing demand for cotton mill machinery. In the case of woolen factories, technical innovations had remained extremely modest, and consequently, machine building for this industry had continued mostly on a small-scale local level. Into the 1820s, home spinning and weaving still commanded two-thirds of the domestic market for woolens. Relatively few machines were needed because the industry remained small and the processes of the woolen mill still relied on traditional craft skills. By 1830, New England's woolen mills included an inventory of machines that was not much advanced from that in the 1790s.

Innovations in Woolen Production

The cornerstones for most mills were their carding machines and spinning jennies. In 1811, the machin-

This illustration of an English spinning jenny, ca. 1809, shows a version of the hand-operated device first patented in 1770. While the Arkwright roller spinning process eclipsed the use of jennies for cotton, jennies remained the principal spinning devices in most woolen mills until the 1830s. *(Source: Abraham Rees,* Cyclopaedia. *Courtesy Slater Mill Historic Site.)*

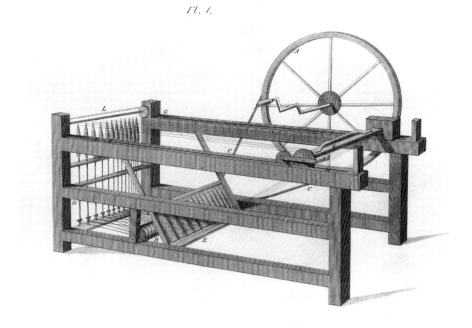

Fig. 1.

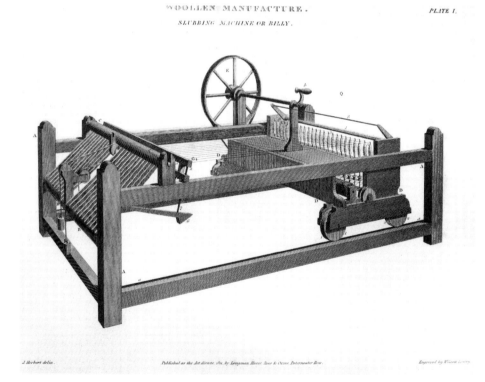

WOOLLEN MANUFACTURE.

SLUBBING MACHINE OR BILLY.

PLATE I.

An English "slubbing" billy is depicted in this engraving, ca. 1809. Using this device, the short wool rolags produced by carding machines were pieced together by children and wound on spindles. This was a bottleneck in woolen manufacture corrected in the mid-1820s by improvements in carding machinery, such as the Goulding condenser. *(Source: Abraham Rees,* Cyclopaedia. *Courtesy Slater Mill Historic Site.)*

Davis and Furber of North Andover, Massachusetts, offered this jack, ca. 1865. *(Courtesy American Textile History Museum.)*

ery in Colonel Humphries's mill in Humphriesville, Connecticut, one of the larger mills of its day, contained only four carding machines and two jennies. A typical mill of 1820 might feature two "sets" of carding machines (three machines in each set) and two hundred jenny spinning spindles. None of this machinery was particularly innovative from a technological standpoint. Improvement of carding and spinning equipment came slowly and the use of newer equipment by smaller mills was uneven at best.

Carding and spinning machines were most often built independently and were not engineered to work together for efficient production. Carding machines designed to support home spinners did not produce material that could be directly used by the jenny or by its improved version, the "jack." Rolags, carded strips of fiber, were produced across the width of the carding machine, the common length being 24 inches. Though this was fine for hand spinning, these two-foot lengths needed to be pieced together with an intermediate tool known as a "slubbing billy" before they could be spun by the jenny. Because of this extra step, jenny spinning remained inefficient, hand spinning remained competitive, and further development of the woolen mills was delayed.

Beginning in the 1820s, New England machin-ists experimented with attachments to the carding machine that could create rolags in endless lengths. John Goulding of Dedham, Massachusetts, produced a "condenser" that created endless rolags along the length of the machines, rather than along the width. Goulding patented his device in 1826, eliminating the slubbing billy altogether, and produced a quantum jump in woolen mill efficiency.

Carding machines with condensers could now produce endless rolags which were wound up on long spools. With no further work, these spools were placed at the feed rollers of the jack. At last, spinning proceeded using carding and spinning machinery designed to work together. In addition, the condenser promoted the use of jacks to replace jennies. Woolen manufacture had moved a step closer to the efficiency of the cotton mill.

"Cassimere" and Its Loom

On a winter's day in 1843, a large sleigh arrived in the yard of the Harrisville Woolen Mill. Carried on this sleigh was one of William Crompton's celebrated "fancy cassimere" looms, the first of these machines to arrive in New Hampshire. Riding with the machine was William Crompton himself who had driven some fifty miles on snow-covered roads

Spinning at the Harrisville Woolen Mill, Harrisville, New Hampshire, is captured in this rare interior photograph, ca. 1880. By this date such jacks were becoming increasingly obsolete as new automatic versions came on the market. When human power was no longer a limiting factor in machine size, spinning machines could be larger and could operate with more spindles. *(Photo by D. S. Rice. Courtesy American Textile History Museum.)*

from Worcester, Massachusetts, where the machine building company of Phelps and Bickford was building the looms under a royalty agreement. This was an important day for the Harrisville Woolen Mill. Indeed, this machine proved important for all woolen mills. The U.S. Commission on Patents would later note that "upon the Crompton loom, or looms based on it, are woven every yard of fancy cloth in the world."[2]

Gaining popularity in Europe and America, cassimere, the fabric made on the Crompton loom, secured its character by weaving subtle patterns on the cloth's surface. Using four-harness looms, twills and herringbone patterns could be produced. French craftsmen applied the jacquard mechanism to this process, creating elegant woven designs in woolen cloth. Since virtually any design could be produced, according to the weaver's fancy, these cloths became known as "fancy" cassimeres.

As with the evolution of other looms used in New England woolen mills, the loom used for cassimere was first intended to serve the cotton industry. But Crompton's visit to Lowell had drawn little interest from the cotton producers. When, however, an example of European fancy cassimere came to the attention of Samuel Lawrence, agent for the Middlesex Woolen Mill, he remembered this earlier visit from Crompton and invited him back to Lowell to rebuild his loom, this time to weave wool. The experiment was a success and the Middlesex Company pioneered a new product, fancy cassimere, which was neither handwoven nor made with the jacquard mechanism. Cassimere soon became a centerpiece for fashion design, replacing broadcloth as the premier luxury fabric for men's fashion.

Cassimeres and flannels soon emerged as all-woolen products that could be woven on power looms. These new lightweight twill cloths required

Daguerreotype of a man seated by a finisher carding machine, ca. 1855. Carding employed a sequence of three machines. The second (intermediate) card delivered carded stock, wound on short spools (seen here at right). The third or "finisher" card (shown in the foreground) delivered rolags wound continuously on long spools, ready for spinning on the jack. *(Courtesy American Textile History Museum.)*

looms with at least four harnesses. The use of multiple harnesses and multiple shuttle boxes in the early 1840s was a step toward the development of the "fancy" loom. These innovations unleashed an unprecedented diversity of woolen cloth designs.

Encouraged by New England machine improvements, woolen mills spread more rapidly throughout the region in the 1830s and building machinery for these mills became a large-scale enterprise. These included the shops as Somersworth, New Hampshire, and Ware, Massachusetts. The area around Worcester, Massachusetts, had a greater-than-average

Wool spinning was photographed in an unidentified small Maine woolen mill, ca. 1910. Here a simple ninteenth-century jack is still in use. *(Courtesy Maine State Museum.)*

number of home spinners and weavers, and this fact may have contributed to the emergence of the city as a major center for the production of woolen machinery on a national scale. Firms such as Gilbert, Gleason and Davis (Samuel Cooper's employer) produced a full range of machinery. Between 1841 and 1845, this company alone produced some 225 carding machines, 206 jacks and 354 looms.

These machine builders differed from their cousins in nearby cotton mill machine shops in several ways. They were not spin-offs from a parent manufacturing company and their products were available directly to everyone on a first-come, first-served basis. The accounts of Gilbert, Gleason and Davis show that their products were used at the same time by both the largest and the smallest mills throughout the region, from Andover and North Andover, Massachusetts, to Dexter, Maine. Small rural mills competed regionally for business by making the same products and using the same machinery as much larger mills.

Chapter 13

The Beginnings
of Social Change:
The New England
Mill Workers

Sally Rice had procrastinated before writing to her parents in February of 1845, because she knew they would disapprove of her actions. After working as a domestic servant in a Union Village, New York, home since 1838, she had left to work in a cotton mill in Thompson, Connecticut. Knowing that her father in Vermont was "dolefully prejudiced against a Cotton Factory," Sally argued that the cotton factory job would pay higher wages (likely), and require less wear and tear on her clothes (unlikely). She had learned weaving by running two looms under supervision, then progressed to running three. Writing to her parents, she expressed the hope that she would get four looms by the end of the year, and then "make more."[1] Instead, by the end of the year, Sally had left the mill and returned to the housework in the Waters family home. Like so many girls and young women from New England farms, Sally had given the mills a try and had briefly been part of the large transient population of mill "operatives" who moved from farm to factory and back to the farm again during the 1820s to the 1850s. For most of these girls, a stay in the mills averaged less than two years.

Back in 1790, Samuel Slater's workforce had consisted of local children. Although the employment of children would later be characterized as a national disgrace, this practice drew little notice in eighteenth-century New England. Here generations of farm families had depended on the labor of the entire household, including children. When Almy, Brown and Slater's new mill was built in 1793, children twelve to thirteen years of age and older dominated the work force. This pattern of staffing was common to all spinning mills built under the Rhode Island system before the introduction of power loom weaving in 1817. While the spinning mule required the skill and strength of adult men,

Rows of roving frames and spinning machines created long "alleys." Here young laborers work to replace filled bobbins and empty spools. The job of moving the bobbins and spools from machine to machine was often the first assignment given to inexperienced mill workers. This interior shot is from the Continental Mill, Lewiston, Maine, ca. 1875. *(Courtesy Maine Historic Preservation Commission.)*

most tasks attending to the Arkwright-type drawing and spinning machines required little skill and relatively little physical effort.

Child and Family Labor

Cotton mills did not invent child labor, but they brought it from the home to the factory. Children faced a long day of relatively easy work, periods of idleness punctuated by shorter periods of rapid work: moving bobbins and cans of yarn and roving, bringing the finished products of each machine to the next in sequence. As a former bobbin girl recollected,

> I can see myself now, racing down the alley, between the spinning frames, carrying in front of me a bobbin box bigger than I was. These mites had to be swift . . . so as not to keep the spinning frames stopped long, and they worked only about fifteen minutes every hour. The rest of the time was their

own, and when the overseer was kind they were allowed to read, knit, or even to go outside the mill-yard to play.[2]

Young Smith Wilkinson's job of tending the carding machine was as difficult as any and more dangerous than most. He describes it in 1835:

> The mode of laying the cotton was by hand, taking up a handful, and pulling it apart with both hands, and shifting it all to the right hand, to get the staple of the cotton straight, and fix the handful, so as to hold if firm, and then applying it to the surface of the breaker, moving the hand horizontally across the card to and fro, until the cotton was fully prepared.[3]

With the change of venue from home to factory came a level of regimentation seldom seen in any eighteenth-century activity. Hours of work at home were long but flexible, the work task-driven, not governed by clocks, bells, or whistles. The orderly

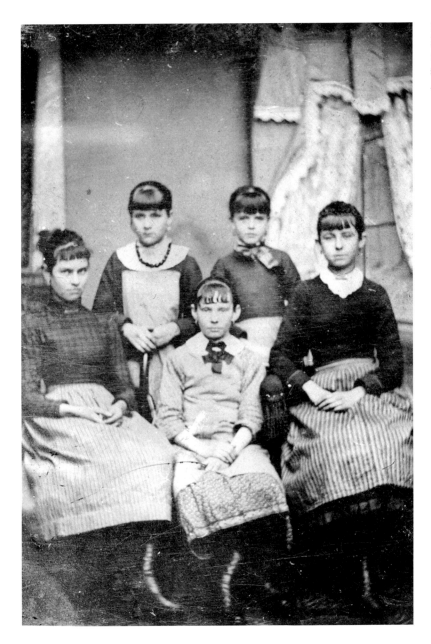

Five "doffer" girls, ca. 1880. Commonly handled by adolescent girls and boys, the task of removing filled bobbins and empty spools was called "doffing." *(Courtesy American Textile History Museum.)*

process of running a sequence of related machines in a factory demanded strict regulation. In the spinning mill, the role of labor was often to handle the stock between the work of each machine. The stoppage of one machine could mean the exhaustion of supplies needed for the machines later in the process or the accumulation of products from the preceding machinery.

Though the workload was not oppressive, the days were long. Soon parents of Slater's workers complained that there was no time left for the edu-

cation of their children. In response to this criticism, Slater introduced "sabbath schools," providing basic education every Sunday.

The newly established mills required an entire village to house the people who would be needed to run them. Commenting about Ware, Massachusetts, Zachariah Allen noted in 1826 that there were "five hundred inhabitants where four years go there were not twenty."[4] Another writer noted that "In the most rocky and desolate locations . . . there is a waterfall. . . . Here factories are erected in this barren waste, and suddenly a large population is gathered."[5] Families were needed to occupy these towns and to provide labor within walking distance of the mills. Sometimes it was necessary for the mill owners to advertise:

> April 25, 1822
> Wanted, a family of six or eight persons to work in a Cotton mill, near this town. Two of them must be Spinners; and the remainder work in the Carding Room. None need apply unless well recommended, and are willing to comply to good and necessary regulations: to such a Family liberal wages will be paid, either in cash or otherwise as may be agreed upon.[6]

Owner/Worker Relations

Cotton mills unquestionably exploited the poverty that was endemic in rural New England. But the chance to earn cash wages led many families to find considerable benefit in factory work. Since it was presumed that all family members would have to work anyway, the benefits of factory work were clear to owners like Smith Wilkinson: "The wages of the family," he noted, "are usually increased, by the addition of children, to from 450 to 600 dollars. They all live better than before."[7] Comments like this can be characterized as self-interested rationalizations. But cotton manufacturers supported hundreds of factory villages and this fact, in itself, testifies to the appeal of a factory option in a sometimes bleak environment of limited choices.

So long as the industry kept expanding, labor was in short supply. Smith Wilkinson, writing in 1831, pointed out: "Our greatest difficulty at present is a want of females, women and children; and from the great number of factories now building, have my fears that we shall not all be able to operate all our machinery another year."[8] Because there was competition for laborers, mill owners established services and amenities ranging from garden plots to company stores to attract and retain transient working families. When times were good, workers would freely relocate in search of a better situation. But,

conversely, bad business conditions could lead to the temporary closing of the mill.

There was little security and little loyalty in most relationships between mill owners and working families. Alexis de Tocqueville saw this clearly, noting in 1840:

> The manufacturer asks nothing of the workman than his labor; the workman nothing but his wages. The one contracts no obligation to protect, nor the other to defend; they are not permanently connected by habit or duty.[9]

Since all the income from members of a large family might come from one mill, a shutdown could prove ruinous. Jobs for many family members did increase family income, but dependency on the mill undermined family security and options. Despite the claims of mill owners, the life of the mill village was sometimes risky and the economic downturn at the end of the War of 1812, and depressed conditions in 1829, in 1837, and beyond, demonstrated the vulnerability of the labor pool tied to the mill village. "In too many cases," a Woonsocket, Rhode Island, historian wrote in 1876, "the manufacturers had lost sight of the human being who operated their machines, and they too often mistook injustice and cruelty for order and discipline."[10]

Female Labor

Women and girls were part of the factory system from the beginning. Until the first use of power looms in Waltham in 1814, cotton yarn was sent out for weaving in family homes where it was mostly a female workforce that produced cloth on a piecework basis. Home weaving of cotton cloth continued well into the 1820s, but with the introduction of the Waltham power loom in 1814 and the "crank" loom beginning in 1817, mills everywhere brought women weavers to the mill. Since young women had been weaving in family homes, it seemed logical that they would be most adept at doing it in the factory. The use of power looms

Three girls posed in a spinning room, possibly the Amoskeag Manufacturing Company in Manchester, New Hampshire, ca. 1905.
(Courtesy American Textile History Museum.)

Tintype of two women in their smocks, photographed to show workers in their textile mill environment, ca. 1880s. *(Courtesy American Textile History Museum.)*

ended the commercial production of cloth in homes, but it created many new jobs for women in the mills. Beginning in Waltham and continuing everywhere, women dominated the work forces of all cotton mills, providing nearly two-thirds of the factory labor. Advice given by a Rhode Island manufacturer in 1824 suggested that a mill of two thousand spindles would need a workforce of fifty girls, ten men, and twenty boys.

The mills at Waltham and Lowell were noted for their use of women as the principal source of labor. The operation of power looms did not demand the extensive experience of mule spinning, but it did require skills not generally found among the chil-

dren of farm families. Especially in the larger corporation cities of northern New England, unmarried young women provided the bulk of the labor.

Women were drawn to factory jobs for several reasons. For the first time, girls and women had the opportunity to earn real cash wages and to do so in their own right. Earning between $2.50 and $3 a week, sometimes more, girls could usually save money even after paying room and board of about $1.25 a week. The money earned was usually money they could keep or spend as they wished. To earn this, the average weaver might produce between ten and twelve yards of cloth per day.

Relocation to places like Lowell was an especially

Weaving was among the highest paid and most well-respected positions for women in mills. As seen in this photograph, ca. 1860, weavers often posed with their shuttles, symbols of their high status within the mill. *(Courtesy American Textile History Museum.)*

Many of Lowell's "mill girls" consciously rejected farm life. In an 1858 article titled "Farming in New England," the point is clearly made:

> The most intelligent and enterprising of the farmers' daughters become school-teachers, or tenders of shops, or factory girls. They contemn [*sic*] the calling of their father, and will nine times out of ten, marry a mechanic in preference to a farmer. They know that marrying a farmer is serious business. They remember their worn-out mothers.[13]

Eventually, Sally Rice, who refused to live on a farm in the mountains of Vermont, married an engineer and settled down to a comfortable middle-class life in Worcester.

These two unidentified weavers are believed to have worked at a Maine cotton mill, ca. 1870. *(Courtesy Maine State Museum.)*

appealing option for adolescents anxious to escape the isolation and parental control of rural life. According to testimony collected by the Massachusetts General Assembly in the mid 1840s: "Nine-tenths of the factory population of Lowell came from the country. They were farmers' daughters."[11] The most common occupation for young women in this period was domestic service, but this offered little prospect for independence or adventure.

Sally Rice displayed a somewhat common adolescent rejection of her parents' life when she wrote home to Vermont in 1839:

> No one knows how much I suffered the ten weeks that I was at home. I never can be happy there in among so many mountains . . . and as for mayyring [*sic*] and settling in that wilderness I wont, and if a person ever expects to take comfort it is while they are young I feel so.[12]

Chapter 14

"Acres of Girlhood": A Workforce of Women

For many young women, work in factory cities like Lowell was expected to be strictly temporary—something they would do just once, early in their lives. For women, this sojourn was an initiation, equivalent to young men going out to sea.[1] The 1845 *Massachusetts Report on the Hours of Labor* noted: "After an absence of a few years, having laid by a few hundred dollars, they depart for their homes, get married, settle down in life, and become the heads of families."[2]

Hiring young single women posed some new problems for corporations and led to some new rules. Owners knew they could not attract young women unless they offered them a "respectable" and secure living and working environment. In Waltham, the Boston Manufacturing Company found women within families, already living in the immediate area, capable of working in the factory. But in the construction of Lowell where a labor pool was not as accessible, boardinghouses, which served as "dormitories" for young unmarried women, were planned right from the start.

The first corporation housing resembled housing in the mill villages of Rhode Island. In Dover, New Hampshire, as early as 1825, houses were being leased to individuals who would manage them under the company's rules, creating a boardinghouse system. In Lowell, the corporation insisted that boarding in corporation housing was a prerequisite for working in its mills. Here, the company could monitor and enforce rules ranging from mandatory curfews to regular church attendance. Visitors to the new factory city encountered an urban/industrial environment like none they had seen before. John Greenleaf Whittier characterized the city as "acres of girlhood, beauty reckoned by the square mile."[3]

With the development of photography people were often photographed in their work environment. The few documented examples of women employed in New England's textile mills are usually posed studio shots rather than candid photos. This tintype image of a woman holding a shuttle and a bobbin was taken around 1875. *(Courtesy American Textile History Museum.)*

Boardinghouse Rules

Corporation-owned boardinghouses favored by many working women. B life helped create a sense of commu mill's female labor pool. And it was probably the peer pressure within the cramped boardinghouses that monitored young women's behavior, rather than the rules. The extension of corporation rules to their after-hours was not appreciated by the independent-minded women who were making their escape from parental control. The rules were no doubt often broken and only about three-quarters of Lowell's female workers adhered strictly to the mandatory rule of living in company housing. In Lowell and elsewhere, all workers did much to shape their environment—within or outside of the rules.

The situation in the larger corporation communities in New England is reflected in the mill town of Saco, Maine. Here men were employed as machinists, loom fixers, laborers, and operators of some machinery. But the bulk of the work fell to girls, mostly between the ages of fifteen and twenty-five. In 1840, the population of Saco had a majority of females: 2,553 women and girls; 1,855 males. Near the mills on "Factory Island," the working girls and women lived either at home, in local families, or

The idyllic park-like setting of early Lowell, with the Merrimack Manufacturing Company in the distance and boardinghouses along Dutton Street, as romanticized in 1849 on the cover of the *New England Offering*. *(Source: Cover illustration for the New England Offering. Courtesy American Textile History Museum.)*

When these four women weavers posed with their shuttles at a Winthrop, Maine, mill around 1860, they also showcased their clothing. Dressed in their finest, they displayed the current fashion in New England. *(Courtesy American Textile History Museum.)*

Woman drawing in yarns in a loom harness at the Pacific Mills in Lawrence, Massachusetts. This was as an early-twentieth-century promotional shot. *(Courtesy American Textile History Museum.)*

Residents posed outside a Pepperell Manufacturing Company boardinghouse, Biddeford, Maine, ca. 1875. This boardinghouse was 420 feet long, four stories high, and contained 256 rooms. *(Photo by A. D. Bonney. Courtesy Maine Historic Preservation Commission.)*

more often in housing units built adjacent to the mills. This company's housing, variously described as tenements, boardinghouses, or blocks, was supervised by older women as it was in Lowell.

The conditions were considered good, but crowded. Privacy was in short supply. A rare peek inside a large corporation boardinghouse was provided in a letter written home from Lawrence, Massachusetts, in 1851:

Imagine to yourselves a girl just entered her twenty-fifth year seated at a small light-stand with writing utensils before her and endeavoring to write a few of her uppermost thoughts near a window that overlooks the principal street in Lawrence in the fourth story of a long brick factory boarding block, with [ten?] beds situated on the east side of the room with a lot of old dresses & skirts hung up behind them & some where in the vicinity of six trunks on the west & south side of the room & a closet filled to overflowing, say nothing about the band boxes & carpet bags these

with a couple of looking glasses and a chair comprise the contents that contains your daughter & sister . . ."[4]

One exaggerated positive report was provided by a Lowell visiting committee in 1845:

The rooms are large and well lighted, the temperature is comfortable, and in most of the window sills were numerous shrubs and plants, such as geraniums, roses, and numerous varieties of cactus. These were the pets of the factory girls.[5]

In 1840, Saco, Maine, had twenty-six "boarding housekeepers" installed in various houses, managing 222 women between the ages of fifteen and twenty, and 264 women between twenty and thirty. The number of women per house ranged from twelve to twenty-five, with Mrs. Mary Day running a particularly large house of fifty-six. The company wished a greater percentage of the help to live in their

Worker housing at the Pepperell Manufacturing Company in Biddeford, Maine, served the needs of single workers until it was demolished in 1910. By then, workers were whole families from French Canada, needing different kinds of housing. *(Photo by B. F. Cole. Courtesy Maine Historic Preservation Commission.)*

Two unidentified women weavers, ca. 1865. It was common practice for young women to pose for the camera with the distinctive tool of their craft, the shuttle. *(Courtesy American Textile History Museum.)*

boardinghouses and, in 1841, when the York Mill sought to insist on this, a mini-strike resulted.

Company Rules and Grievances on Both Sides

> All persons in the employ of the Hamilton Manufacturing Company, are to observe the regulations of the room where they are employed. They are not to be absent from their work without the consent of the overseer, except in cases of sickness, and then they are to send him word of the cause of their absence. They are to board in one of the houses of the company and give information at the counting house, where they board, when they begin, or, whenever they change their boarding place; and are to observe the regulations of their boardinghouse.[6]

These were part of the stipulations of the Hamilton Manufacturing Company. The rules governing work and housing were established by mill owners and always reflected the interests of the company. The posted rules were a catalog of the owners' needs and wishes, not necessarily an accurate reflection of everyday life. Corporations expected workers to stay for at least a year, for example, and to give two weeks notice before leaving. Yet the company did not guarantee to keep employees employed for the term of one year. The tyranny of the work schedule was among the frequent labor complaints. One Lowell woman wrote in 1841:

> I am going home, where I shall not be obliged to rise so early in the morning, nor be dragged about by the factory bell. . . . Up before day at the clang of the bell, and out of the mill by the clang of the bell . . . and at work in obedience to that ding-dong of a bell.[7]

In fact, the stays in Lowell factories were relatively short. Men averaged just over two years, while half of the women stayed less than one year.[8] When these terms were violated, reemployment was supposed to be difficult, if not impossible. But absences were frequent, and many girls left and returned to the same mill after taking a couple of months off

This rare group of tintype photographs is a "class" picture, showing the employees of the carding room at Mill No. 5, Amoskeag Manufacturing Company, Manchester, New Hampshire. *(Courtesy Manchester Historic Association.)*

Rules and Regulations
TO BE
OBSERVED BY THE HELP IN THE MILL.

The hands must commence work at the hoisting of the Gate.
In coming into the Mill every person must go direct to their own room.
Every person is expected to attend to their own business, and avoid all unnecessary debates.
Every person is required to keep their own machine clean and in good order.
Any person using a tool belonging to the Mill, must see that it is returned to its proper place.
Any person damaging any tools or fixtures belonging to the Mill, will be expected to replace them.
No person allowed in the Finishing Room excepting those employed there.
All persons are strictly prohibited from meddling with the Steam Valves, excepting the overseer of the room.
No person allowed in the Mill on the Sabbath.
No work of any description allowed to be done in the Mill on the Sabbath.
The Hands are particularly requested to avoid swearing or the use of profane language.
Those wishing to leave are required to give two weeks notice to the overseer.
The overseer is expected to see that these regulations are observed.

"Rules and Regulations" were posted in most mills. This example is believed to originate from the Stevens Mill in North Andover, Massachusetts, in the nineteenth century. While the rules were frequently ignored, many workers resented the company's paternalism. *(Courtesy American Textile History Museum.)*

A plain backdrop and a floor covering provided photographers with a studio setting within the mill in this tintype photo of a weaver, ca. 1865, whose shuttle is a source of professional pride. *(Courtesy American Textile History Museum.)*

and returning home. As long as labor was relatively scarce, workers exercised some control and were often granted some latitude.

On the other hand, employers complained of the lack of discipline in the work force. Andrew Ure, writing in 1835, took the mill owner's perspective, arguing that:

> To devise and administer a successful code of factory discipline, suited to the necessities of factory diligence, was a Herculean enterprise. . . . It is found nearly impossible to convert persons past the age of puberty, whether drawn from the rural

or the handicraft occupations, into useful factory hands. After struggling for a while to conquer their listless or restive habits, they either renounce their employment spontaneously, or are dismissed by the overlookers on account of inattention.[9]

Mill agents and overseers also had some cause for complaint. The 1829 diary of the agent N. B. Gordon of the Union Cotton and Woolen Manufactory in Manville, Connecticut, depicts his frustration when work was interrupted by sickness, machine breakdowns, bad weather, family emergencies, and a variety of other excuses. On January 7, two weavers were sick and at least some looms were stopped for sickness on five other days that month. When a cut in wages was announced, the whole mill was shut down by angry workers.

In 1839, the mill was back at work, but Gordon still had to cope with ongoing labor problems. On February 4, he noted that he had "a poor lot of weavers at this time." On February 8, it snowed and Gordon "sent the girls home on a sled." In May, the "picker boy" announced that he was "sick of the mill." Gordon paid him and sent him home. On July 5, Gordon noted that the "warper girl run off last night," and on July 27, "The two White girls come in at noon, made excuse that it was all wet." On October 18, Mary Abbott and Jonah Grant "quit the mill." In December, "all hands, except Bethahr, sick with the mumps."[10]

The Manville mill was a small concern compared with the mills of Lowell and other Waltham-style mills. Infectious illnesses spread more easily in the congested spaces of the boardinghouses and must have hampered operations. Workers in Lowell no doubt had an inventive catalog of excuses as well.

Emancipation of the "Mill Girls"

Although the mill girls did not stay in factories for long, the impact of their new freedom had enormous ramifications for women and eventually for society in general. Mills were filled with intelligent, independent-minded young women anxious to advance themselves. Whereas women had worked in isolation doing household work, the boardinghouse brought together hundreds of like-minded women, forming a community of common experience and interest. Here women suddenly emerged from the shadows of history and demonstrated their capacities outside the household, seizing their new possibilities. Lowell offered them more opportunities and education than had existed at home. Harriet

Robinson, former mill girl, noted in her book *Loom and Spindle*:

> Some of us were fond of reading, and we read all the books we could borrow. One of my mother's boarders, a farmer's daughter from the "State of Maine," had come to Lowell to work, for the express purpose of getting books, usually novels, to read, that she could not find in her native place. She read from two to four volumes a week; and we children used to get them from the circulating library, and return them, for her.[11]

The 1830s saw a flowering of literature in New England and Lowell's mill girls attended lectures at the Lyceum. When the literary magazine, *The Lowell Offering*, was launched, its editor noted that it was "not only the first work written by factory girls, but also the first magazine or journal written exclusively by women in the whole world."

These mill employees were individuals whose lives could not be defined only by their work. Harriet Robinson suggested that these workers be remembered as unique individuals: "When I look back into the factory life of fifty or sixty years ago, I do not see what is call 'a class' of young men and women going to and from their daily work, like so many ants that cannot be distinguished one from another; I see them as individuals, with personalities of their own."[12]

Despite its shortcomings, Lowell was for its first decade an uncommon phenomenon. "Lowell is not amusing," Michael Chevalier wrote in 1836, "but it is neat, decent, peaceful and sage." Of Lowell's mill girls, it must be said that, though the deck was stacked against them in terms of advancement, they were not victims of the factory system. For the most part, they learned how to manipulate their environment and achieve their objectives in the face of the corporation's power. In the mill towns, they received more than what had been offered working at home.

Chapter 15

Rising Tide of Discontent: The Struggle for "Freedom"

David Gillis, agent for Manchester Mills, was standing behind Mayor Theodore Abbott in March 1855 when he was struck in the head by a doughnut. This missile, part of the contents of a worker's lunch pail, was intended for the honorable mayor, who was addressing a crowd of mill workers in an effort to reestablish order in the city of Manchester, New Hampshire. From the workers' point of view, it was merely part of their struggle against the absolute control of the factory owners.

Problems had begun in February when the company announced the return of an eleven-and-three-quarter-hour workday, reversing concessions made to workers during the previous year. With no responses from the company or the city's political leaders, workers rebelled. The women of Manchester Mills were the first to walk out. They were soon joined by workers from the Amoskeag and Stark Mills and, led by a band, they marched around the city carrying banners for their cause.

On the following day, the newly elected mayor, following instructions from the company agents, attempted to disperse the mob by delivering a speech. Using bugles, drums, and other instruments, the band punctuated his remarks with drum beats and dramatic flourishes, which precipitated gales of laughter from the crowd. The humiliated mayor, failing to see the humor, made matters worse when he threatened to arrest the band. Enjoying their roles as comedians, the protesters asked Abbott to produce a copy of the city's statute against music. The workers had little hope of changing the company's policies, but their mocking of the mill agent and the mayor were for the moment a priceless small ripple in what was a rising tide of discontent.[1]

Nineteenth-century industrial development cre-

Workers assembled for a group photograph outside the Stark Mill in Manchester, New Hampshire, ca. 1880s. *(Courtesy Manchester Historic Association.)*

ated many new jobs, but it also redefined the relationships between worker and employer. In many industries, traditional craft skills were replaced by machinery processes, removing the skill from the production of goods and consequently diminishing the value and therefore independence of the workers. It was mostly the skilled artisans who organized into trade unions that represented them communally against the employers. In the expanding textile industry, however, the first widespread labor dissatisfaction in cotton and woolen mills did not come from organized trade organizations or from unions trying to help their members hold on to their jobs. It came directly from the workers.

Defiance in the Ranks

In both large and small factories, the unrest came from the female workforce. There was defiance in the ranks wherever women factory workers forged a community of common interests and values. The first strike or "turn-out" of workers occurred in Pawtucket in 1824. In this action, as well as another in Dover in 1828, and in the 1832 and 1836 walk-outs in Lowell, the ringleaders as well as the strikers were mostly women. If mill owners had imagined that a female workforce would be easier to control, they were in for a shock. Whittier's "acres of girlhood" stunned Lowell's agents and treasurers, who now referred to them as the "Amazons" who fought them in the streets of Pawtucket, Dover, Lowell, Manchester, and anywhere else with a concentration of women workers.

At first, distrust and dissatisfaction between workers and mill agents revolved around the issue of cuts in pay. The agents and mill owners tried, in vain, to argue that business conditions had forced them to make pay cuts. The women, however, noting that the price of cloth had not fallen, quickly dismissed this argument. To the workers, cuts in pay were the clear result of avarice by the owners.

The owners, looking out from their city counting houses, had tried to promote themselves as agents of beneficial social and economic change. But at the work site they were clearly seen as greedy capitalists. Though there were some genuine "bottom line" business realities in the running of a factory, most of the business losses were the direct result of the owners' miscalculations and overextensions. Too much cloth was being made, stockpiles occasionally demanded cutbacks to reduce inventory, and the price of cloth continually fell in response to production levels. The industry had embarked on a cycle of boom and bust—and the workers were the first to pay the price.

A system of hourly wages was created in the mills that altered the relationship between employer and employee and threatened to upset worker independence and equality. The women of Lowell, as they reminded their employers, were "the daughters of freemen." Coming to mill cities from the hardscrabble farms of northern New England, workers brought with them an idealized vision of America: a classless society without the hierarchy of aristocracy. To them, the founding fathers were not distant ancestors, but close relatives in the generation of their parents and grandparents. The unilateral decisions made by their employers reminded them too much of the privileged British nobility whom their ancestors had fought.

Alexis de Tocqueville expressed the sentiment of the age in 1840:

> But for equality, their passion is ardent, insatiable, invincible: They call for equality in freedom; if they cannot obtain that, they still call for equality in slavery. They will endure poverty, servitude, barbarism—but they will not endure aristocracy.[2]

In the faceless power of mill owners the women of Lowell saw emerging a source of authority that threatened the promise of America itself. They were correct in recognizing that manufacturers were becoming the nobility of America, diminishing the promise of the Declaration of Independence. The Boston Associates and other rising manufacturers had become the new elite, and, as such, they did not fit into the popular concept of democracy in America. Working men and women resented the pretensions and power of Boston's "purse-proud aristocrats."

The relationship between the mills' investors and the workers was forever altered by labor conflicts. The era of good feelings and common interest between employers and employees in Lowell had lasted barely a decade. When the Harris mill in Woonsocket burned in 1835, it was reported that a nearby gathering of workers cheered the flames. Woonsocket historian E. Richardson noted in 1876 that this spectacle would not be repeated because the interests of the workers and owners were ultimately the same. But he was wrong. As de Tocqueville observed:

> The aristocracy created by business rarely settles in the midst of the manufacturing population which it directs: the objective is not to govern the population, but to use it. An aristocracy thus constituted can have not great hold upon those it employs; and ever if it succeeds in retaining them at one moment, they escape the next.[3]

"Disturbances" such as the strikes of 1834 and 1836 would probably have continued with regularity if not for the serious depression of 1837 to 1842, which made money even tighter and therefore protest futile. During these years many of the mill girls went home to their farms, and with them went the Revolution-era idealism, now further diminished by the reality of a new wage-earning structure.

Mule spinners worked hard and under difficult conditions but were the highest-paid employees working on the mill floor. To keep humidity levels high, water was frequently spread on the floor of the spinning room and heated from below. Thus many workers in the mule room wore no shoes, as seen in this photograph, ca. 1910. *(Courtesy American Textile History Museum.)*

Technology Affects Workers

With the return of prosperity, issues of democracy and financial remuneration changed to factory working conditions. The effort to limit the length of the working day came to the forefront.

When technology increased the pace of production and made certain tasks for workers obsolete, the quality of life in textile factories began to deteriorate. When the pace of work had been "leisurely" and weaving on the mill floor had been less strenuous, the long workday drew only limited attention and complaint. When water turbines replaced water wheels, the speed of production increased as more horsepower could be generated from the same water flow. More machines could be run in each mill. Spindle speeds became faster, more yarn was produced at a more rapid rate, more bobbins were filled

up faster. The work of supplying bobbins and spools to the speeding machinery became more rigorous. In sum, tending machinery was much more labor-intensive. As the pace of the factory accelerated under the continued drive for corporate profits, the life of the factory worker became more difficult, and workers began to complain about working conditions.

One mill girl had complained in a Manchester, New Hampshire, newspaper that "during the past three months, I have been spoken to three times, for being seen with a book or paper in my hands." As the work of wage-earners in the factory evolved, it could no longer be expected that workers had the leisure to take a break, let alone to read on the job.

To be fair, some of the technological improvement were beneficial to all parties. One such improvement was the development of "stop motions,"

Workers assembled outside a B. B. and R. Knight Mill in Rhode Island, ca. 1910. (*Courtesy Slater Mill Historic Site.*)

which could stop the loom automatically when a yarn was broken. This meant that weavers could manage more looms. Piecework weavers like Sally Rice could "make more," even though the profit of this increase in productivity was distributed unevenly in favor of the owners.

In the 1840s few trades enjoyed a ten-hour work day. Since much work was done on a piecework basis, hours of work were impossible to monitor and not necessarily beneficial to labor. But the dawn-to-dusk schedule of farm work was now a distant memory to most workers, and the demand for shorter hours of work and for parity among manufacturers began to grow. The "ten-hour movement" required negotiations, the support of politicians, and the passage of legislation. For this agenda, the mill girls were at a disadvantage. Without voting rights,

they could only indirectly influence the action. Still, they took the lead, forming the Female Labor Reform Association in Lowell. Along with a similar men's organization, the Lowell Mechanics and Laborers Association, they exercised political pressure.

Politics and Petitions

Other communities were engaged in the struggle as well, and it was the workers of Fall River who first submitted a petition to the Massachusetts Legislature in 1842. The following year, a Lowell petition included sixteen hundred names, and by 1845 the petition was an annual event with growing numbers of signers. Although they could not vote, Lowell women represented three-quarters of the petitioners.

The legislature responded by appointing an investigating committee under the leadership of Representative William Schouler of Lowell, a corporation apologist. Since most of the petitioners had been women, Schouler reasoned that the proposition should be defended by women, thinking they would not be as articulate or strong: "I would inform you that as the greater part of the petitioners are female; it will be necessary for them to make the defense, or we shall be under the necessity of laying it aside."[4]

Schouler called eight witnesses of his choice to testify—six of them women, possibly assuming that they would be intimidated by the prospect. Far from intimidated, Lowell's Sarah Bagley had already responded: "We hold ourselves in readiness at any time." After hearing testimony and making perfunctory mill visits, the committee concluded that legislation was not needed. Not surprised, the Female Labor Reform Association challenged the report and, particularly, chairman Schouler. Determined to defeat him in the next election, the Association pledged to keep him "where he belongs, and not trouble the Boston folks with him."[5] When he was defeated in the fall elections, the FLRA thanked the voters for "consigning William Schouler to the obscurity he most justly deserves."[6] The mill girls may have had no voting rights, but they were not without power.

In 1846, the statewide petition secured more than ten thousand names—four thousand from Lowell alone—but the political power of the owners and financiers made clear that victory would be hard won and would take a long time. The depression of 1847 to 1852 effectively dampened labor agitation. While in New Hampshire and Rhode Island legislation was passed to establish a ten-hour day, these actions were ineffective, since workers could—and did—agree to contracts prescribing longer hours. By 1853, however, the corporation mills adopted an eleven-hour workday, although it was claimed that mill clocks were tampered with and the machinery sped up to make up the loss.

In 1855, the Amoskeag and other Manchester, New Hampshire, mills announced a return to the eleven-and-three-quarter-hour day, prompting widespread work action, the closing of several mills, and the departure from Manchester of thousands of ex-

Boy workers posed for this group photograph at Slatersville, Rhode Island, ca. 1910. *(Courtesy Slater Mill Historic Site.)*

perienced workers—not to mention the ricochet of a doughnut off agent Gillis's head. Though a face-saving compromise was reached, everyone knew the workers had won when Manchester's mill restored the eleven-hour day.

The adoption of a ten-hour day did not come until 1874, thirty years after the Lowell Female Reform Association was founded. But it would be inaccurate to recall the women of the corporation textile mills as victims or failures. To a large degree, they succeeded in their agenda of independence and left a clear mark on history. It was through their struggle to limit working hours and retain their independence that the modern women's movement was first conceived.

As early as the 1840s, Alexis de Tocqueville expressed his admiration for what he saw in the women of America: "For myself, I do not hesitate to vow that . . . to what singular propensity and growing strength of the people ought to be attributed, I should reply: to the superiority of their women."[7]

Chapter 16

"Gifted in Mind, Body and Estate": New England Builds an Immigrant Work Force

Beginning in the 1830s and continuing until the Civil War, work in textile mills grew less appealing to New England farm girls. The growing U.S. economy provided more choices for a young, mobile labor force, while work in the mills was becoming more difficult.

Some sons and daughters of New England farmers continued to join the mills on the same terms as before, but certainly during boom times the mills could not fill their labor needs. From an early date, mills had actively recruited foreign workers for many skilled jobs, including mule spinners and calico printers from England as well as weavers from Scotland. Small populations of these immigrants had appeared, creating ethnic neighborhoods with nicknames such as "John Bull's Row" and "Scotch Block." But it was the immigrants from farming districts in Ireland and Canada who would replace the Yankee farmers' daughters at the spinning frame and the loom.

Early in the nineteenth century, the duress of farming in New England had led workers to factory cities. Beginning in the 1820s, agricultural failures in Ireland and French Canada led these populations to follow the same paths to the mills blazed by members of the New England farming communities. While many Yankee families sought advancement by moving to the American West, waves of agricultural populations came to New England from Ireland and from French Canada.

The Irish

The Irish were the first to arrive, particularly during the years of the great potato famine in the mid 1840s. Later, after the Civil War, immigration grew dramatically from Quebec. Together, the Irish and

Many thousands of textile mill workers came to New England from Quebec, Canada, beginning in the 1860s. This photo of the author's cousin Delianne Aubin (*left*) and Mademoiselle Rousseau, posed with their tools of the trade, was probably taken in Lewiston, Maine, ca. 1880. *(Courtesy Marietta Binette.)*

the French Canadians soon overwhelmingly made up the workforce of New England mills from the 1860s on, defining the social development of these communities to the present day.

Arriving in Boston, the Irish were first employed as laborers in the construction of the canals and mills. One such immigrant, Michael Reddy, walked to Providence in search of work. In 1825 he was hired to work on the digging of the Blackstone Canal and over the next year and a half, "dug his way through . . . to Woonsocket," where he lived for the rest of his life. Irish labor was, in fact, essential

to the building of large textile manufacturing cities throughout New England. Recognizing the important work of the Irish, Woonsocket historian E. Richardson wrote in 1876: "To the thousands of his [Reddy's] fellow countrymen thus gifted in mind, body and estate—to their wit, their muscle and their poverty—the development of our natural resources, and the consequent progress of our nation during the last fifty years, is mainly due."[1]

In the beginning, Irish labor was not used in actual manufacturing. But following the end of the depression of 1837 to 1843 and the 1844 Tariff Act the expansion of textile manufacturing outstripped the labor pool to be found on New England farms. Irish girls began to take their places in the mills, starting with the lowest-skilled, lowest-paying jobs in the carding and spinning rooms. By 1845, 8 percent of the workers at Hamilton Mills in Lowell were immigrants; only five years later it was 33 percent, most of whom were Irish. A decade later, 60 percent of the immigrant workforce was Irish.[2]

The French Canadians

The influx from eastern Canada was like no other mass relocation. The farmers of French Canada were not newcomers to America. Many shared a 250-year heritage with New England Yankees. Living next door to New England, the "French" came to America by train, a short trip through New England that covered relatively few miles but a great social distance. They arrived through New England's open back door. Points of arrival were not Boston or Ellis Island, but the train stations of Biddeford and Lewiston, Woonsocket, Manchester, and many other New England towns where local textile mills provided jobs.

Quebec remained the true home of these new-comers. Like the Yankee girls before them, they too envisioned a short stay at the mills and a return home, their culture intact. Though it was a danger-ous sojourn for French Catholics among Protes-tants, the French language was a useful barrier against the dangers of the melting pot. Many French mill workers returned to Quebec and remained there. Many others made extended return visits to help with family farms during the summer months. Their leaves were sometimes so extensive that some mills like the Pepperell Manufacturing Company in Biddeford, Maine, simply closed for a time.

Relocation of French Canadians in great num-bers took place in mill cities and towns, where their arrival immediately provided a critical population density. This "mass" worked to sustain cultural dis-tinction and values. Yankee girls knew they could return home, and the French Canadians often dreamed they would as well. But since their reloca-tion often resembled a colonization effort, they brought their own society with them. Families often moved together from the same communities, bringing with them an entire support system of common history and values. Like the Irish before them, the French Canadian influx forced important changes in the character of mill cities and towns.

A New Society

Immigration often involved entire families—and the workforce that ran the machinery soon re-flected this. As in the earlier mills of the Rhode Island system, earning money for survival was a shared responsibility for most members of the fam-ily. It was common for the head of the household to work as a laborer, while the wife worked in the home. It was the numerous children and adolescents from age eight to eighteen who had jobs in the mill. The family of Joseph Gilbert, a thirty-seven-year-old laborer, was typical. At home, his wife tended their four small children under the age of seven. But Mary, age sixteen; Joseph, fourteen; Eliza, twelve; and Anna, eight, were all employed in the mills.[3] Under these harsh circumstances education was limited, though the second generation of French Canadian immigrants usually emerged from the experience better educated than their parents had been.

Compared to the independent-minded and vocal Yankee mill girls, the immigrants were more tract-able. No longer did the mill owners seek control through boardinghouses, nor were the boarding-houses appropriate to house whole families. As mill towns became a workforce of immigrants, the "be-nevolent" paternalism of the company also dimin-ished. While a native-born mill girl had complained to a Manchester paper that she had been "spoken to" about carrying a book with her, few of the new immigrant employees would have had the audacity to imagine that work in the mill would allow for reading on the job. Immigrant workers were far more grateful to leave the uncertainty and near star-vation of their immediate past. Most immigrants stayed in the mill towns. For most Irish, immigra-

A group of immigrant weavers from Sweden, photographed in Manchester, New Hampshire, in the 1880s. *(Courtesy Manchester Historic Association.)*

tion had been a one-way ticket; for most French Canadians, the difficult economic conditions awaiting them at home prevented their return for decades.

Cultural pluralism in New England was rooted in the region's nineteenth-century textile mills, mill villages, and factory towns that had arisen amid the fields of the Yankee farmers. As pockets of Irish, French Canadians, and many other immigrant groups gathered at mill gates, the character of New England was forever changed. A new society of diverse language, culture, class, and religion resisted the power of the vaunted American melting pot. Inevitably, the history of New England became part of the heritage of its newest citizens. The enduring legacy of the once-great New England textile industry still lives on in communities where today local phone books and census roles list family names that first appeared in two thousand textile mill payroll offices.

Chapter 17

The Lawrence Experience: The Fall and Reprise of a New England Textile City

The most heart-rending calamity of the age will forever distinguish the Tenth Day of January, 1860. On that day, at thirteen minutes before five o'clock, in the afternoon, the Pemberton Mill, in Lawrence, Mass., fell to the ground without a moment's warning, and buried a large number of operatives in the ruins.[1]

At six o'clock in the evening of January 10, 1860, the news of the collapse of the Pemberton Mill was sent out to the world through a dispatch from the Associated Press: "One of the most terrible catastrophes on record occurred in this city, this afternoon." The word spread rapidly. On January 21, 1860, an illustration of the collapse appeared on the cover of *Harper's Weekly* and by January 24 nearly twenty thousand dollars had been raised to provide relief for the injured and their families.

Led by a five-thousand-dollar gift from the New England Society for the Promotion of Manufactures, the list of contributions included five dollars from "a Laborer, Holyoke," and some two thousand dollars contributed by "the Citizens of Providence," Rhode Island. The sense of community among factory workers was inspiring. "Operatives of New Market Manufacturing Company," in Newmarket, New Hampshire, collected $263.90 in donations. Workers from textile mills throughout the region—Nashua, Manchester, Holyoke, Andover, Biddeford, Salem—joined together in raising funds.[2]

For the Boston Associates, it was a public relations disaster, from which they would never fully recover. But the Pemberton tragedy was just the last and most graphic of the setbacks faced by the Boston plutocracy in the decade of the 1850s. The Boston Associates had lost $10 million in their early development of Lawrence and Holyoke. For the general public in America, there was great sadness arising

This rendering of the destruction of the Pemberton Mill was drawn from a photograph taken at the scene. A version of the same image was used to illustrate the cover of *Harper's Weekly* on June 21, 1860. *(Courtesy American Textile History Museum.)*

from the loss of the Pemberton Mill and its employees, but virtually no sympathy for the loss of the owners' millions.

Conspicuously absent from the roster of donors among the cotton and woolen mills of the region during the first two weeks following the Pemberton disaster were any of the factories in either Lawrence or Lowell owned by the Boston Associates. A two-thousand-dollar gift from the Suffolk Club in Boston may have represented a contribution from the Associates, but the owners certainly kept a low profile.

Disasters in Lawrence and Holyoke—
Financial and Otherwise

The building of the mill town of Lawrence had been a notable engineering achievement and it en-

joyed its share of success. But both Lawrence and Holyoke, conceived in the 1840s, endured many business setbacks in their early days arising from forces beyond the control of promoters, owners, and labor.

The Boston-based investors had always been cautious. Anxious to keep the development of cotton mills "in the family," they initiated growth in the communities over which they could exercise almost total control. The "development" of Lowell, for example, continued for nearly twenty years. The Boston Associates also absorbed their financially strapped imitators, owning and reorganizing mills they had not launched. Thus, the early mills at Dover, Somersworth, Saco, Biddeford, Nashua, and Manchester fell into the hands of a relatively small group of Boston investors.

Meanwhile, by the 1840s there were thirty-two mills at work in Lowell and the development of that city was for the moment complete. Some of the investors, notably Abbot Lawrence, were drawn to the idea of building an even bigger and better textile manufacturing city. They chose a site overlooking the Merrimack River some eleven miles below Lowell. Here waterpower estimated at eleven thousand horsepower could be harnessed by building the largest dam yet attempted on the Merrimack River: a granite arc thirty-six feet high and nine hundred feet long.

Under the supervision of the Essex Company's chief engineer and superintendent, Charles Bigelow, Irish laborers dug canals. The Atlantic Cotton Mills and the nine-story Bay State Mills were built, along with the large, beautiful Lawrence Machine Shop.

But the timing for such major expansion couldn't have been worse. The years of sustained profit in cotton manufacturing were ending just as the new city was rising, and mills in Lawrence simply added to the overexpansion. In 1850 the coarse sheeting favored by northern Waltham-style mills was selling at 7 percent below cost. A decade later, the Essex Company was still pleading with its stockholders to be patient, but confessing that "the stockholders will see, therefore, that we do no business which brings a profit, that only a small portion of our property produces an income, and that we have a very large property entirely unproductive."[3]

At the same time, prior investment in the large-scale system of dams and canals had presumed continued expansion. When Abbott Lawrence and his few Boston partners could find no takers for their new mill sites, they developed the mills themselves. While retrenchment might have been prudent, Lawrence's investors were actually forced to expand. The Pacific Mills (1852) and the Pemberton (1854) were underwritten by Lawrence to keep the machine shop at work. His personal investment in the new city bearing his name soon reached one million dollars—and in the 1850s that was serious money.

Previous business depressions, like the Panic of 1829, had driven many of the Boston Associates' upstart competitors out of business. This time, however, the Associates did not profit from depression but were stung by it. The crisis of 1857 could not be covered up with more growth activity. The Pemberton, the Bay State Mills, and the Lawrence Machine Shop all declared bankruptcy with a loss of $4.5 million, while the Essex and Pacific companies lost another $1.5 million. In Lawrence alone, the loss to the Boston Associates totaled $6 million.

Parallel to the Lawrence experience, the city of Holyoke was established at Hadley Falls. Here a two-thousand-foot dam was built initially of wood, but when it was immediately swept away by the weight of the water, it was rebuilt in stone. The Holyoke dam was meant to power as many as twenty-five mills, but by 1850 only the two Lyman Mills were using it. In 1857 the Hadley Falls Company went bankrupt. With $3 million in assets, the company's property sold at auction for only $325,000. The financial disasters at Lawrence and Holyoke raised questions about the prudence of the Boston elite.

An All-Time Low for Boston Associates

The Boston Associates had always had their detractors. As early as 1826, Zachariah Allen had written of the development of Ware, Massachusetts, that it was "all forced hot bed growth of Boston capital" that would not survive "longer than those who have the funds are willing to disburse them to please their fancy for manufacturing."[4] After the failure of the Pacific Mill, Allen felt empowered to level a personal criticism of Abbott Lawrence, writing: "Dearly did he pay for this vainglorious indulgence of his pride."[5]

The Boston elite had never confused philanthropy with business. In pursuit of their own interests, success had often come at the expense of others. When, for example, they decided to raise the level of the dam in Lowell, they first sold their upstream mill property in Nashua—doubtless aware that their action would raise the water level between Nashua and Lowell and cause water to pond up below the wheels upstream. Now, in the 1850s, few tears were shed when the mighty Boston Associates fell.

Lithograph of the Lawrence Machine Shop, Lawrence, Massachusetts, 1854–1859. Built of fieldstone, this structure remains one of the most handsome factory buildings ever constructed in New England. *(Courtesy American Textile History Museum.)*

The losses at Lawrence and Holyoke, the collapse of the Holyoke dam, and the tragic fall of the Pemberton Mill were blows to the Boston elite. The Boston Associates had lost a lot of money, but the collapse of the Pemberton mill galvanized public opinion against them. Although the inquiry into the disaster concluded that it was most likely caused by faulty cast iron columns, public opinion blamed the collapse on corporate greed and indifference. Without waiting for the evidence, *Harper's Weekly* concluded eleven days after the disaster: "Society is unanimous in its verdict on the terrible disaster in Lawrence, everyone denounces the builder and the proprietors of Pemberton Mills."[6]

It is, however, evidence of their vast wealth and power that the Boston Associates still managed to survive and prosper. The growth envisioned for Lawrence and New England did ultimately take place. In 1860, most of New England's large-scale mill cities were yet to be built or to achieve their

potential. In places like Lawrence and Holyoke, the largest growth was yet to come. As often happens, great wealth managed to buy immunity from the usual consequences of miscalculation and incompetence.

Worsted Woolens and the Reprise of Lawrence

After its 1860 disaster, Lawrence experienced a reversal in fortune largely due to the city's preeminence in the manufacture of worsted wool. Worsteds rapidly became the standard for finer clothing made for both men and women. And Lawrence became the worsted capital of the world.

Both woolen and worsted cloth are made from sheep's wool, but the fiber preparation process for each is very different. For the spinning of woolen yarn, carding encourages the intermixing and entanglement of the curly fibers. For worsted yarn, the objective is to lay the fibers straight and parallel through the process of combing, rather than carding. Combed worsted combines many of the benefits found in both wool and cotton. Lighter yarns are possible and these can be spun using machinery similar to that used in the cotton industry.

Efforts to mechanize the combing process had been underway in England and France beginning in the 1830s. But combing machines were totally unknown in America, and even in Europe hand combing was still common into the early 1850s. In 1853, Pacific Mills in Lawrence entered the business and imported the first combing machines in New England. Using supplies of both cotton and wool, worsted manufacture became the source of Lawrence's growth and success.

The impact of worsted production began in the 1830s with the import of a new fabric called "delaine," short for the French *mousseline de laine*, or wool muslin. Using cotton for warp yarns and worsted for filling, this thin cloth was frequently printed like cotton calico, the rage for summer dresses in the decades of the 1830s and 1840s. Like satinet, delaine could be woven on power looms designed for cotton. Although the experience in New England with wool combing was limited, manufacturers were anxious to give delaine a try.

Delaine was first produced in the Ballardvale Mill in Andover, Massachusetts, rented by Abraham Marland. Here the wool was combed by hand and the woven cloth sent first to nearby North Andover to be printed using hand blocks and later to the Hamilton Mill in Lowell or in Fall River to be printed on roller presses. Marland's modest effort was soon matched by the work of the original Amoskeag Company of Manchester, New Hampshire, at the initiative of Rhode Island investors including Samuel Slater.

Worsted manufactures expanded by leaps and bounds. By 1868, there was more than two million yards of worsted cloth being made on the Merrimack River—a half million in Lawrence alone. The original Bay State Mills were reopened as Washington Mills and it was here that the first "merino worsted coatings" were made in the late 1860s using French combs. These were copies of cloths exhibited at the Paris Exposition of 1867 and they were so successful that they sold on the American market as French goods. The Arlington Mill, which opened in 1865, reorganized as a worsted mill in 1867. It included both worsted and cotton departments and produced a large variety of high-quality dress goods.

In the years that lay ahead, worsted manufacture would continue to expand in Lawrence and would culminate in the construction of the largest worsted mill in the world. Neither Abbott nor Amos Lawrence lived to see the triumph of the city they had launched, but only its downfall. Lawrence had risen from its ashes and become one of the major textile manufacturing cities in the world.

Chapter 18

Smokestacks and Train Tracks: Steam Engines Promote Textile Manufacture

"Old Abe" and "the Honorable Joe" were not friends. In fact, they were lifelong competitors. The one, Abraham Howland, sailed on New Bedford whale ships, served in the Massachusetts legislature and lost a bid for Congress in 1848. The other, Joseph Grinnell, grew up in a whaling family and won a seat in Congress by defeating Old Abe in 1848. Both these men played critical roles in leading New Bedford away from its single-minded focus on whaling.

In 1846, Abraham Howland incorporated a cotton mill that might provide employment "of which," as Nathaniel Parker Willis pointed out, "the families of sailors and mechanics could avail themselves, independent of the precarious yield from the sea."[1] Raising the capital from the city's elite whaling families proved impossible for Howland and would not be easy for Grinnell either. In the 1840s, New Bedford was the nation's foremost whaling center, serving as home port to more than 250 whaling ships. Few in New Bedford realized just how precarious a business whaling would become after oil was discovered in 1859. The heyday of the whaling industry would pass quickly under a flood of kerosene. In order to survive and prosper, New Bedford would need to reinvent itself to become the foremost cotton-manufacturing city in America. This would be made possible by yet another invention: the steam engine.

With the engineering achievement of the steam engine, steam power emerged as a groundbreaking alternative to waterpower. First developed in England in the late eighteenth century, the promise of the steam engine to replace waterwheels was not immediately recognized. Eventually, however, this new invention would create a source of power with revolutionary consequences, promoting the spread of textile manufacture in New England even fur-

The Naumkeag Steam Mill in Newburyport, Massachusetts, is depicted in this oil painting, ca. 1850. The introduction of steam engines meant that mills like this could be built in seacoast cities with an abundant labor pool and access to shipping routes. *(Courtesy American Textile History Museum.)*

ther. Doing the same work as waterwheels, steam engines casting their trail of smoke on the urban horizon could drive textile mills and do it without proximity to rivers and streams. When mounted on wheels, the engine was transformed into a locomotive, opening the use of large inland waterpower sites through the train lines. Together, smokestacks and train tracks were signals of the great industrial prosperity in mid-nineteenth-century New England.

The Effects of the Steam Engine on the Textile Industry

Compared to the region's abundant waterpower, the high cost of buying and maintaining steam engines inhibited their use. But these engines offered an advantage that was increasingly important as the pursuit of waterpower drove manufacturing to distant and remote regions. Steam engines could be placed anywhere. Dams or canals no longer rooted the industry to any fixed site. Most significantly for textile producers, steam engines allowed mills to move to locations where labor was abundant. As a writer in *Niles Weekly Register* pointed out in 1835: "It is cheaper to use steam power in the midst of a dense population, than to use water power, which often makes it necessary not only to build a factory, but a town also."[2]

Samuel Slater demonstrated the promise of the steam engine as a power source for textile mills when he established the Providence Steam Manufacturing Company in 1827. Now the mills of the Blackstone Valley could move downstream to the sea. At this time, the development of waterpower

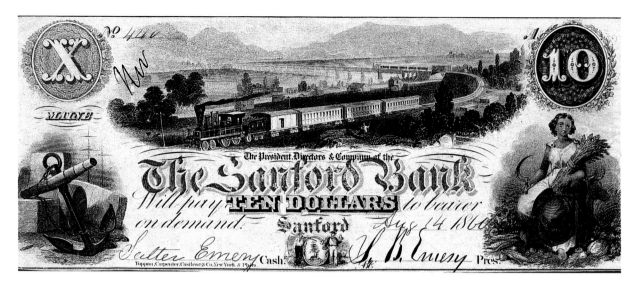

This banknote, issued by the Sanford (Maine) Bank in 1860, features an engraving of a locomotive and train. The arrival of rail lines was a sign of promising community growth and prosperity. *(Courtesy Maine State Museum.)*

still remained the clear choice of New England manufacturers. Once canals and mills were built, the waterpower was virtually free.

Steam engines, however, made good sense for the ironworking and machine-building industries. Not surprisingly, smokestacks—the first sign of steam power—appeared in textile centers around the machine shops and foundries. Builders of engines and boilers for steamboats and locomotives, these industries already imported coal. Lowell and Lawrence were great manufacturing centers founded on the use of waterpower, but even here the Lowell Machine Shop and the Lawrence Machine shop were run by steam.

Large investments in the development of waterpower continued through the 1840s and 1850s and continued to a second phase of growth, with investments in Lawrence and Holyoke, Massachusetts, as well as Brunswick, Augusta, and Lewiston, Maine, in the late 1840s, the 1850s and the 1860s. But by the Civil War further expansion was diminishing markedly. Meanwhile, steam mills were being built along the coast to the north of Boston in Salem and Portsmouth, New Hampshire, and particularly in Newburyport. In these communities, cotton mills could find workers from the families of seamen and fishermen for whom few other working options existed.

Early steam engines had difficulties with regulating speed. Power needed to be adjusted to respond to changes in the load. This problem was eliminated with the development of an "improved" engine invented and manufactured by George Corliss of Providence. The Corliss engine was a spectacular success and led the way in the steam powering of many New England textile mills. Many of Corliss's engines were undoubtedly shipped by steamboat to Fall River where they helped transform a relatively small concentration of cotton mills into national leadership.

Seaside Mill Towns

The waterpower of Fall River was conveniently located near the sea, even though the available power was limited. The opportunities for development did not match the large-scale aspirations of Lowell, Holyoke, Manchester, and Lawrence, and so the Boston financiers were not interested. Fall River continued to be part of the greater Providence–Narragansett Bay economic orbit. By 1850, when waterpower development was still expanding in the Merrimack Valley, New Hampshire, and Maine, the power of the Quequechan in Fall River was already used up.

Yet these relatively small Rhode Island–style villages were to explode to the forefront of cotton manufacturing in New England. In the decade of the 1860s, Fall River rivaled Lowell, and by 1875 the new "spindle city" was twice the size of Lowell. With over 1.8 million cotton spindles at work, Fall River took its turn as America's largest textile center, a position second in the world only to Manchester, England, in the mid-1870s. In 1875, though there were still 11 waterwheels at work yielding over 1,000 horsepower, this use of power was dwarfed by the city's 81 steam engines, which produced nearly 28,000 horsepower.

Fall River had been "discovered" during the initial spurt of expansion from Pawtucket between 1807 and 1814. The impetus came with the help of merchants and mechanics from the Pawtucket/Providence area, particularly those who had worked for Slater. In Fall River, development began with a cotton mill built by Job Durfee in 1811 and with the building of the "Old Yellow Mill" by David Anthony, a former Slater employee, and his cousin Dexter Wheeler. The town, then known as "Troy," featured a series of eight falls on the Quequechan River.

Originally owned solely by the Borden family, this waterpower was developed principally by three families: Borden, Durfee, and Chace. By 1845, six

cotton mills, an ironworks and two calico printing mills were located here—and these used up all the available power of the river. The second phase of Fall River's development would rely on the power of steam engines. Coal was already delivered to Fall River for domestic use and for the ironworks, which was the first to employ steam. Growth was rapid. Between 1863 and 1868, eight new companies were launched, and some twenty-two new mills in 1871 and 1872 alone. By 1876, Fall River had forty-three factories producing yarn to serve more than thirty thousand looms.

Nearby New Bedford was a logical place for the construction of steam-driven cotton mills, but textile manufacture came late to this city. With more than 250 whale ships in a fleet of some seven hundred ships in its harbor in the 1840s, New Bedford was a major national port. Although there was an abundant labor pool—some ten thousand residents of the city were sailors—the profits from the sea had long created wealth, jobs, and world fame. When Abraham Howland incorporated Wamsutta Mills in 1846, he found that he could not secure the needed investment from the city's merchant elite who were quite satisfied with the nearly ten-million-dollars-worth of whale oil and whalebone brought into harbor each year. The corporation was taken over

New Bedford's first cotton mill, Wamsutta, as pictured on a cloth label. (*Courtesy American Textile History Museum.*)

Once railroads provided access around the falls at Brunswick, mills appeared along the Androscoggin River in Lewiston, Maine. This picture was taken around 1875. *(Courtesy Maine Historic Preservation Commission.)*

The Pepperell Manufacturing Company of Biddeford, Maine, ca. 1875. *(Courtesy Maine Historic Preservation Commission.)*

by Joseph Grinnell. Firmly established in the city merchant elite, Joseph Grinell was able to raised the needed funds to establish New Bedford's first successful cotton mill, and the only one for twenty-four years. Here, as Nathaniel Parker Willis wrote, "a sailor's daughter, for example (who else might be painfully dependent, or compelled to leave home and go out to service), may earn four dollars a week by independent and undegrading labor."[3]

Whaling was still center-stage in New Bedford and no other mills were started until 1871. Instead of establishing more companies, Wamsutta just grew bigger and bigger using more and larger steam engines. By 1889, Wamsutta alone featured one Corliss engine of three hundred horsepower, a pair of engines producing eight hundred horsepower, another pair generating one thousand horsepower, and the "monster pair" of two thousand horsepower—

larger than the celebrated engine that ran all the exhibits at the 1876 Exposition. In the twentieth century, the former whaling capital emerged as the largest cotton manufacturing city in America.

The products of both Fall River and New Bedford featured the finer shirting and sheeting favored by the Rhode Island mills. The dampness of the coastal climate aided in the spinning and weaving of finer counts of yarn. Wamsutta, in particular, established a name-brand recognition that was thought to add as much as two cents a yard to its sale value. In 1876, "percale" sheets were introduced and became a standard for quality right up to the present day.

Using waterpower, many New England mill cities had been created from a wilderness. Steam engines, however, could be put anywhere, and this flexibility held the potential to adversely redefine communi-

A large grouping of cotton mills in Manchester, New Hampshire, was depicted in this oil painting, ca. 1875. *(Courtesy Manchester Historic Association.)*

The Continental Mill in Lewiston, Maine, as seen in this photograph ca. 1875, was a celebrated architectural achievement. *(Courtesy American Textile History Museum.)*

ties that already had developed other personalities. Steam power also brought with it some negatives. The development of large waterpower had demanded a master plan of dam, canal, and city design, but steam-driven mills imposed no such order to the landscape. By 1875, Fall River had some twelve thousand corporation-built housing units and many more were built by private investors. Without a grand scheme of development, a declining quality of urban life faced a workforce increasingly composed of immigrants.

The Effect of Railroads on the Textile Industry

Stationary steam engines led textile manufacture downstream to the seacoast and inland to districts lacking waterpower. At the same time, these engines were being made into locomotives, fostering the development of remote upstream waterpowered sites previously overlooked or avoided. The Boston Associates were quick to recognize the importance of railroads to their investments. In addition to the Middlesex Canal, Lowell could be connected to Boston by rail lines. In 1832, the Locks and Canals Company imported two Stephenson "Planet" locomotives. Their Lowell machinists studied these engines to produce clones of their own and, in 1835, the company's machine shop produced eight more engines.

Another phase in waterpower development was fostered by the railroads. Lewiston, Maine, became a prime example of a city of waterpower made possible by steam locomotives. Here the waterpower of the Androscoggin was among the best in Maine, but as late as the 1840s it was barely used for any kind of manufacturing. Viewing the developments in Massachusetts and at Saco, several leading citizens, particularly Edward Little, sought to develop Lewiston's power in the same fashion. But Lewiston was geographically isolated and the economic viability of this development plan came with the promise of rail traffic. Here, as elsewhere, the railroad made business possible, and with the trains came Boston investors and Boston money. The Lewiston Water Power Company, like its predecessors elsewhere, assumed a broad development role that ranged from dam and canal construction to the building of machinery and cotton mills. Later organized as the Franklin Company, the Water Power Company managed, between 1850 and 1870, the most aggressive cotton mill development in Maine. It also built some of the largest cotton mills yet constructed in New England.

Under the leadership of Boston capitalists, particularly Thomas Hill and Benjamin Bates, the Water Power Company began the systematic development of the waterpower and the construction of canals in 1850. In that same year, both Hill and Bates incorporated their own cotton manufacturing companies to directly assume operations of several mill sites. The Bates Manufacturing Company com-

menced operation two years later. The following year, 1853, saw the addition of Lewiston Mills. In 1854, the Hill Manufacturing Company opened its new mill, and the Franklin Company developed Lincoln Mill in the late 1850s as well. Androscoggin Mills was built in 1860 and by 1866 Continental Mills opened its truly massive structure.

By now the great period of mill construction was nearly over. In a span of just fourteen years from the commencement of the Bates Manufacturing Company to the completion of Continental Mills, the small rural town of Lewiston saw the construction of eight cotton mills, employing thirty-three waterwheels to drive 220,000 cotton spindles. In the years just after the Civil War, it employed over 1,500 men and 3,500 women.

By the time that the Lewiston Water Power Company began its development, the American cotton industry was in a mature stage of development. The development of Lewiston was no longer an experiment. Lewiston's turn came relatively late, but the mills constructed were among the largest and most modern built anywhere in New England. Railroads permitted the exploitation of the Androscoggin at Lewiston, but the rise of the city, along with that of Fall River and New Bedford, was dependent on an immigrant labor pool by then composed largely of French Canadians, who would give these cities a particular character that still remains.

Chapter 19

Speeders, Pickers, and Mules: New England's New Machinery

Detail of a mill wheel. *(Photo by Anton Grassl. Courtesy American Textile History Museum.)*

The productivity of the Great Falls Manufacturing Company in Somersworth, New Hampshire, stunned the manufacturers at Waltham and Lowell. Soon after it opened, this cotton mill was producing 30 percent more cloth than any of its sister mills. This was a triumph for Rhode Island mechanic Asa Arnold, who later recalled the proud moment when his work "brought down the directors of the Lowell corporations to our place."[1] No doubt, he particularly enjoyed explaining to Moody and the others "the minutiae of a Rhode Island invention."[2] Top mechanics from Lowell who had earlier rejected Arnold's invention came to Somersworth to see for themselves what was going on. They also sent the celebrated mathematician Mr. Warren Colburn to check things out. When Colburn told Paul Moody, superintendent of the Lowell Machine Shop, that Arnold's device was "mathematically correct," a shirtsleeves Rhode Island mechanic had, for the moment, out-engineered the Massachusetts corporate Goliath.

Asa Arnold demonstrated the practical uses of a differential gear he had invented in 1818, a gear used today in the rear axles of almost every car in the world. He also demonstrated the ongoing leadership of Rhode Island machine-building genius. Rhode Island mechanics had pioneered the building of textile machinery for nearly twenty-five years before the first of the Boston Associates' mills had been built. They provided a critical mass of skilled, experienced machinists whose expertise could often be traced to the Pawtucket, Rhode Island, area. Pawtucket Falls had provided a fertile climate for the birth of the coming machine age.

James S. Brown's "Patent Speeder" was produced in Pawtucket by one of Rhode Island's premier machine shops. James's father, Sylvanus, had built woodwork for Slater's first machines in 1789 and 1790. *(Source: James Geldard,* Cotton Manufacture. *Courtesy American Textile History Museum.)*

At the start, this was a small world in which the principal mechanics all knew each other. Here, near the old Slater Mill, the first generation of New England textile machine builders thrived as the new industry grew. The Wilkinsons, builders of a wide assortment of machinery including the Gilmore power loom, worked next door to the old Slater Mill. Asa Arnold worked directly across the river at Slater's White Mill, while Larned Pitcher and Ira Gay built machinery within walking distance. These men, plus many others—including Perez Peck, Daniel Anthony, and Arnold Olney—helped form the first "school" of New England machine builders. Later, they would fan out to other machine shops, carrying the seeds first planted in Pawtucket.

Since they had all been active participants in creating the new machine-building industry, they sometimes believed the textile business rightfully belonged to Rhode Island. The influx of Boston capital, beginning in 1814, was a threat and sometimes an insult to them. Many no doubt agreed with Zachariah Allen's criticism of Nathan Appleton, principal Boston investor in Waltham and Lowell, that he had "traveled out of his way to sneer at the less fortunate Mr. Wilkinson and his poorer fellow manufacturers in Rhode Island."[3]

The Era of Machine Shops

As Boston investors tried to clone the success of Waltham and then Lowell, they turned to the mechanics of Rhode Island to manage their machine shops. There was a major "brain drain" from Rhode Island to the Boston corporation mills and shops. Asa Arnold eventually went to Somersworth, Ira Gay ran the machine shop in Nashua, and Arnold Olney managed the shop in Ware.

Following the death of Francis Cabot Lowell in 1817, the Boston Manufacturing Company embarked on a strategy of patenting the line of machinery it built and then licensing the use of its patents, as well as selling machinery. As other Boston investors outside the original circle invested in cotton manufacturing they were compelled to pay for the right to use machine designs. Investors in the cotton

The locomotive engine *Amoskeag* was made by the Amoskeag Machine Shop in Manchester, New Hampshire, in 1853. *(Courtesy Manchester Historic Association.)*

mill in Dover, New Hampshire, in 1821, paid $6,000 for the use of the Waltham patents for five years. The Rhode Island pioneer machinery builders resented this aggressive approach by the well-funded, upstart company. Samuel Slater summed up this opinion when he complained: "A certain cotton manufacturing company, who have been in the business only a few years, have pretended to be the inventors of almost everything and have taken out patents accordingly."[4]

The machine shops built by the Boston Associates held the inside track on the machine business generated by the corporation's mills. In Saco, Maine, for example, even before the corporation's large wooden mill was completed, a machine shop was built to produce some 735 separate machines needed for the new mill, including 224 spinning frames, 300 power looms and 120 carding machines.

Despite their advantages, at first the corporation machine shops could not dominate the machine-building business. After all, the cornerstone tool of all machine shops, the slide-rest lathe, had been developed by David Wilkinson in 1794 in Rhode Island. In an era characterized by rapid technological change, "invention" was a great equalizer among mechanics and machine shops. Good ideas could, and did, come from many sources. Even in the face of Boston money, important innovations continued to spring from the work of less well-financed Rhode Island mechanics: Arnold's differential superseded Lowell's "double speeder," Wilkinson's Gilmore power loom supplanted the Waltham/Lowell power loom, and "ring spinning," invented by John Thorpe in Pawtucket eventually replaced most throttle spinning machines in both Europe and America.

In Rhode Island shops, patents were usually secured and awarded to the individual inventors—and this may have contributed to an uncommon level of inventiveness there. Meanwhile, in shops like those in Lowell, patents were secured in the name of the corporation or by the shop's lead mechanic. This practice tended to inflate the reputation of Lowell's Paul Moody, patentee of almost everything developed in his shop, and of the Lowell Machine

This "throstle" spinning machine, built by the Locks and Canals Company/Lowell Machine Shop, from 1825 to about 1835, was found in Biddeford, Maine, and is on view at the American Textile History Museum. Lowell's investors built, sold, and licensed machinery like this. While many products made by the Lowell Machine Shop were derived from earlier English patents, machines produced under the supervision of chief machinist Paul Moody were always elegantly built and well engineered. *(Courtesy American Textile History Museum.)*

Shop. Since individual corporation machinists may not have shared in the profits of their inventions, the initiative to invent was likely diminished.

Eventually, the evolution of the machine-building business favored the larger, well-funded shops. Precision tools became increasingly important because parts needed to be interchangeable and engineered to allow faster machine speeds. The cost of outfitting a first-class machine shop grew beyond the capacity of most small-time operators. Here, the

corporation mills had a distinct advantage. Without question, surviving machines built in either Lowell or Saco in the 1830s display elegant, high-quality engineering.

Corporation machine shops flourished as textile machine shops became laboratories for development of most of the high-tech mechanical innovations of the early nineteenth century. The shops of Lowell, Lawrence, Taunton, and Manchester all built locomotives, putting on the rails many classic

This steam fire pumper was made by the Amoskeag Machine Shop in Manchester, New Hampshire, which produced more than five hundred pumpers between 1859 and 1876. *(Courtesy Manchester Historic Association.)*

examples of the American locomotive that would open up the West. The Amoskeag shop in Manchester built some 550 steam fire engines between 1859 and 1876, while also making architectural columns, fire hydrants, sewing machines, and even cast-iron streetlights for the city. When the armored Civil War ship the *Monitor* was built, the moving turret was machined at the Lowell Machine Shop. Along the way, machinists throughout New England helped lead the development of precision machine tools. Thus, the textile industry created the modern machine tool industry.

Locomotive engines were the high-tech leaders of the mid-nineteenth century. In New England, they were often built by textile mill machine shops. The *Abbott Lawrence*, shown here, was a passenger engine produced by the Lawrence Machine Shop, ca. 1854–1859. *(Courtesy American Textile History Museum.)*

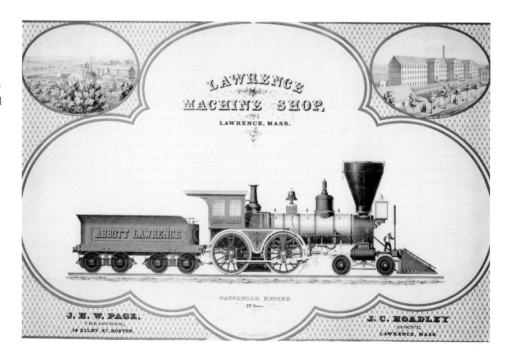

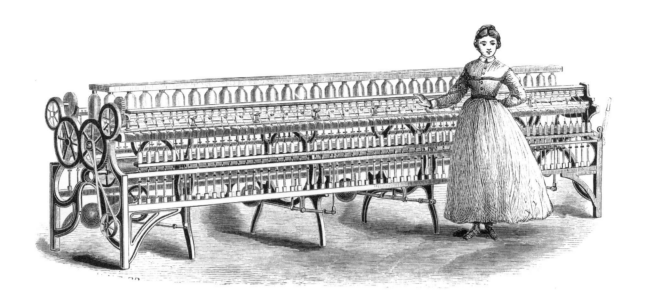

This 1845 promotional illustration depicts a Fales and Jenks spinning frame from Pawtucket, Rhode Island. *(Source: James Geldard,* Cotton Manufacture. *Courtesy American Textile History Museum.)*

The Era of Business Management

Machine building had emerged as a separate branch of manufacturing. The cost of specialized machine tools demanded that machine builders have shops of their own, distinct from any particular mill site. Eventually this led the way to the end of the era of clever mechanics and to the beginning of an era of business management. By the 1840s, men like David Wilkinson—first-rate mechanics but third-rate businessmen—became fossils of an earlier age. Again, Boston capital held a distinct advantage.

The transition was easily made by many of the northern corporation mill shops, notably those at Lowell, Lawrence, Manchester, and Saco, where corporate business structure had first supplanted unstructured creativity. It was also made by machine-building companies in Rhode Island, reborn after the Panic of 1829, such as Fales and Jenks of Pawtucket. While inventor-initiated machine building was far from over, a new kind of machine-making enterprise was emerging. More closely managed and highly structured, these businesses often lacked the freewheeling creativity that had characterized earlier work. Instead, these modern firms used man-

agement strengths to improve and market new ideas from all possible sources. Two firms, Whitin and Draper, became dominant in New England. Together with Fales and Jenks and Saco-Lowell, these builders best illustrate the larger, wide-ranging machine-building enterprises leading into the twentieth century.

The Whitin Machine Company had its roots in the 1830s, when John C. Whitin, son of founder Paul Whitin, developed a new picker. Whitin's Improved Picker was patented in 1832 and first sold in 1834. The success of the Whitin Machine Works did not depend on new inventions under its control. It reacted quickly to change, embraced and improved new machinery, adapted the work of others, produced new inventions, bought patent rights, and abandoned product lines when it could not compete with the products of competitors. The company produced virtually any machine needed in the industry. Once a builder of John Whitin's picker, the company ultimately abandoned this product altogether when a superior machine was introduced by William Kitson.

Whitin's improved version of the "Rabbeth" spindle was widely used, but the company's greatest

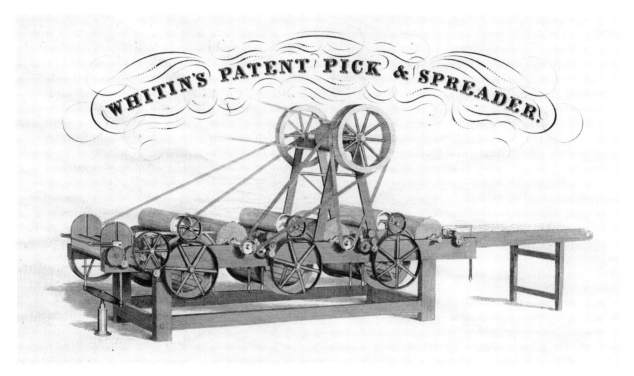

Whitin's Patent Pick and Spreader helped launch a New England machine-building giant of international importance in Whitinsville, Massachusetts. *(Courtesy American Textile History Museum.)*

Advertising illustrations such as this one from the 1890s helped promote the broad woolen/worsted loom made by the Crompton Loom Works in Worcester, Massachusetts. *(Courtesy American Textile History Museum.)*

technological achievement was the Whitin cotton comber. With productivity double that of any other cotton comb, it drove all competitors from the market. With an interior plant size of over twenty-six acres in Whitinsville, Massachusetts, and more acres in the foundry, Whitin was one of the largest machine builders in New England by the end of the century. Its only rival was the Draper Company, located just a few miles away in Hopedale, Massachusetts.

New Machinery Markets

In terms of working plant area, Draper was arguably New England's largest machine builder. With nearly thirty acres of shops, Draper employed some three thousand men at its height. This company originated as early as 1816, when Ira Draper patented an improved loom temple, a device mounted on looms to hold the edges of the cloth apart at a uniform width. In 1842, son E. D. Draper moved the company to the community of Hopedale, for years considered a model of factory town development. When a superior spindle was developed for ring spinning in 1871 by Jacob H. Sawyer, George Draper improved it, and by the early twentieth century the company had sold over 32 million. Purchasing the American rights to the "automatic" Northrop loom, Draper soon dominated the market for cotton looms.

Even when New England's cotton industry began its decline, machine builders continued to build and market machinery near the ancestral home of the American textile industry. Within just a few miles of each other along the Blackstone Valley corridor south of Worcester, the giant machine shops of Whitin and Draper stood in the neighborhood of the old pioneer mills. Nearby in Worcester, Crompton and Knowles dominated the production

The Draper Model "A" (also known as the Northrop Loom) revolutionized weaving in American cotton mills by introducing a system to automatically change empty shuttle bobbins while the loom continued to run. Here a Draper Model "A" Loom arrives in Greenville, South Carolina, ca. 1890s. *(Courtesy American Textile History Museum.)*

The "Knowles Fancy Loom" became the standard for worldwide weaving of worsted and woolens in the late 1860s. This loom was the result of several improvements to the Crompton loom made and patented by Lucius Knowles. In 1892, the Knowles and Crompton companies, both of Worcester, Massachusetts, merged to form Crompton and Knowles, which would dominate the weaving of woolens and worsted through the 1960s. *(Courtesy American Textile History Museum.)*

A "ring twister" advertised with this lithograph was made by the North Andover, Massachusetts, machine builders Davis and Furber. *(Courtesy American Textile History Museum.)*

Man posed in front of roving frames, ca. early twentieth century. *(Courtesy American Textile History Museum.)*

of woolen and worsted looms, and in North Andover, Davis and Furber excelled in making woolen-carding machinery. But the products of Whitinsville, Hopedale, and even Pawtucket were now heading south, where they would help launch the textile industry in places such as Greenville and Spartanburg, South Carolina, and Greensboro and Gastonia, North Carolina.

Back in 1845, James Montgomery, an agent for the York Manufacturing Company in Saco, had criticized the older Rhode Island mills for their continued use of machinery that he found "old and dirty." Now, as the nineteenth century was coming to an end, much of the machinery capitalized with the building of New England mills was "old," if not "dirty." Stockholders, a more sedate ownership than

Workers posed for this picture in a carding room early in the twentieth century. *(Courtesy American Textile History Museum.)*

the original innovative investors, opted for immediate profits rather than longer-term investment. Burdened by aging factories and equipment, the owners held on to their income as long as possible and rarely took the risks needed to lead. The spirited entrepreneurs who spearheaded the Boston Associates' era were gone.

In the old New England mill towns, old machinery now awaited the interest of museum curators. Obsolete machinery came to the attention of the Smithsonian, the Henry Ford Museum, Lowell National Park, and the American Textile History Museum. As the newer products of New England machine building headed south to the new center of American textile production, the golden age of New England textile production slipped slowly below the horizon. And the once proud equipment of the fledgling textile industry—the spinning wheels, the hand looms, even the jennies—became objects for contemplative historic interest.

NOTES

1. INTRODUCTION

1. Martha Ballard's diary, excerpted in *The History of Augusta* (Augusta: Charles E. Nash & Sons, 1904).

2. Moses Greenleaf, *A Survey of the State of Maine in Reference to Its Geographical Features, Statistics and Political Economy* (1829; reprint, Augusta: Maine State Museum, 1970), p. 277.

3. *Niles Register*, 1828.

2. EXTEND THE MILLS

1. Paul E. Rivard, "Textile Experiments in Rhode Island, 1788–1789," *Rhode Island History* 33 (1974): 35–45.

2. *Providence Gazette*, 8 August 1789.

3. Moses Brown to Samuel Slater, Almy, Brown and Slater Papers, Rhode Island Historical Society Library.

4. Erastus Richardson, *History of Woonsocket* (Woonsocket: S. S. Foss, 1876), p. 126.

3. THE "MASHEEN"

1. See Martha Ballard's diary in Nash.

2. Quoted in Armstrong, *Factory Under the Elms*.

3. *Somerset Recorder*, 1879.

4. MADE IN FAMILIES

1. Blackstone Manufacturing Company "Account Books," Rhode Island Historical Society Library.

2. David J. Jeremy, *Transatlantic Industrial Revolution: The Diffusion of Textile Technologies Between Britain and America, 1790–1830.* (Cambridge, Mass.: M.I.T. Press, 1981), p. 220.

3. Bureau of the Census, *Returns for Alfred, Maine, 1850.* Microfilm in Maine State Archives.

4. Carleton Woolen Mill, "Account Book" (Alna, Maine). Copy in Osborne Library, American Textile History Museum.

5. DIAPER, TOW, AND CRASH

1. Henry Coleman, "Notes by the Way," *New England Farmer*, 18 November 1835. Quoted in *All Sorts of Good Sufficient Cloth*, p. 27.

2. Moses Davis diary (Edgecomb, Maine). Microfilm copy in Maine State Archives.

3. *All Sorts of Good Sufficient Cloth*, p. 15.

4. Ibid., p. 27.

6. GREAT EXPECTATIONS

1. American Home Missionary Society, "Manufacturing Communities and Villages" (*New Englander* 7, No. 2, May 1849) published in Steve Dunwell, *Run of the Mill* (Boston: David R. Godine, 1978), p. 69.

2. George S. White, *Memoir of Samuel Slater* (Philadelphia: Printed at 46 Carpenter Street, 1836), p. 191.

3. Thomas Steere, *History of the Town of Smithfield* (Providence, E. L. Freeman & Co., 1881), p. 92.

4. T. Throstle, "Factory Life in New England," *Knickerbocker Magazine* 30 (December 1844): 516. Published in Dunwell, p. 71.

5. Quoted in Steve Dunwell, *Run of the Mill* (Boston: David R. Godine, 1978), p. 71.

6. Quoted in Dunwell, p. 14.

7. White, p. 130.

8. Ibid.

9. American History Workshop, "The Fall River Source Book" (Report for the Master Plan and Design

of the Fall River Heritage Park, 1981), p. 401. Copy in
Osborne Library, American Textile History Museum.

   10. Richardson, p. 168.

   11. Quoted in Dunwell, p. 77.

   12. White, p. 131.

   13. American History Workshop, p. 401.

7. THE WALTHAM POWER LOOM

   1. Published in Kulik, Gary, Roger Parks and Theodore Z. Penn, eds. *The New England Mill Village, 1790–
1860* (Cambridge, Mass.: M.I.T. Press; North Andover,
Mass.: Merrimack Valley Textile Museum, 1982), p. 147.

8. "THE BEST WHEEL IN THE WORLD"

   1. Kirk Boott Diary, 4 September 1823. Quoted in
Dunwell, p. 38.

   2. Deposition, U.S. Circuit Court, *Tyler v. Wilkinson*,
found in Federal Records Center, Waltham, Massachusetts.

   3. Ibid.

   4. Ibid. Deposition of Moses Brown.

   5. Richardson, pp. 125–26.

9. GENIUS, WEALTH, AND INDUSTRY

   1. Quoted in Dunwell, p. 35.

   2. Michael Chevalier, *Society, Manners, and Politics in
the United States* (Boston: Weeks, Jordan & Company,
1839), p. 143.

10. CALICO, BLOCKS, AND ROLLERS

   1. William R. Bagnall, *The Textile Industries of the
United States* (Reprint of 1893 edition. New York:
Augustus M. Kelley, 1971), quoted in Jeremy, p. 110.

   2. John Williams to William Shimmins, 19 August
1825. Quoted in Jeremy, p. 110.

   3. Ibid. Quoted in Jeremy, p. 108.

   4. Ibid.

   5. Potter, p. 572.

   6. Diane Fagan Affleck, *Just New from the Mills* (North

Andover, Mass.: Museum of American Textile History),
p. 11.

11. "SIMPLY PREPOSTEROUS"

   1. J. R. Cole, *History of Tolland County, Connecticut*
(New York: W. W. Preston & Co., 1888), p. 815.

   2. J. Hayes, *History of the City of Lawrence* (Lawrence:
E. D. Green), p. 153.

   3. Arthur Harrison Cole, *The American Wool Manufacture* (Cambridge: Harvard University Press, 1926), note 1,
p. 65.

   4. *Eastern Argus*, May 1804.

   5. A. H. Cole, vol. I, p. 153.

   6. Hayes, p. 153.

   7. Ibid., p. 143.

12. JENNY, JACK, AND BILLY

   1. Gilbert, Gleason & Davis, account book, 1841.
Osborne Library, American Textile History Museum.

   2. Quoted in "Crompton Loom Works" catalog, Osborne Library, American Textile History Museum.

13. THE BEGINNINGS OF SOCIAL CHANGE

   1. Kulik, p. 389.

   2. Thomas Dublin, *Women at Work: The Transformation
of Work and Community in Lowell, Massachusetts, 1826–1860*
(New York: Columbia University Press, 1979), p. 69.

   3. Kulik, p. 64.

   4. Candee, p. 32.

   5. Dunwell, p. 69.

   6. Kulik, p. 409.

   7. Kulik, p. 172.

   8. Ibid.

   9. de Tocqueville, vol. II, p. 172.

   10. Richardson, p. 171.

   11. Robert H. Bremner, ed., *Children and Youth in
America, Vol. I: 1600–1865* (Cambridge, Mass.: Harvard
University Press, 1970), p. 597.

   12. Kulik, p. 388.

   13. Dublin, p. 55.

14. "ACRES OF GIRLHOOD"

1. Carl Russell Fish. *The Rise of the Common Man, 1830–1850* (New York: The Macmillan Company, 1927), p. 89.

2. Bremmer, p. 597.

3. Lawrence F. Gross, *The Course of Industrial Decline: The Boott Cotton Mills of Lowell, Massachusetts, 1835–1955* (Baltimore: Johns Hopkins University Press, 2000), p. 19.

4. To "friends at home," from "Ann," June 1851. Osborne Library, American Textile History Museum.

5. Bremmer, p. 598.

6. Ibid., p. 599.

7. Dunwell, p. 49.

8. Dublin, p. 55.

9. Gross, p. 9.

10. Dublin, p. 87.

11. Bremmer, p. 606.

12. Ibid., p. 602.

15. RISING TIDE OF DISCONTENT

1. James P. Hanlan, *The Working Population of Manchester, New Hampshire 1840–1886* (Ann Arbor: UMI Research Press, 1981), pp. 72–73.

2. de Tocqueville, vol. II, p. 103.

3. Ibid., p. 172.

4. Dublin, p. 114.

5. Ibid., p. 115.

6. Ibid.

7. de Tocqueville, vol. II, p. 227.

16. "GIFTED IN MIND, BODY AND ESTATE"

1. Richardson, p. 164.

2. Dublin, p. 147.

3. 1870 Industrial Census, Lewiston, Maine.

17. THE LAWRENCE EXPERIENCE

1. *An Authentic History of the Lawrence Calamity*, 1860.

2. Ibid.

3. *Lawrence up to Date, 1845–1895* (Lawrence: Rushforth & Donoghue), p. 20.

4. Candee, p. 32.

5. Dunwell, p. 88.

6. Ibid., p. 91.

18. SMOKE STACKS AND TRAIN TRACKS

1. Henry Beetle Hough, *Wamsutta of New Bedford* (New Bedford: The Vineyard Gazette, 1946), p. 28.

2. Dunwell, p. 105.

3. Hough, p. 28.

19. SPEEDERS, PICKERS, AND MULES

1. Kulik, p. 134,

2. Ibid.

3. Ibid., p. 148.

4. Ibid.

SELECTED BIBLIOGRAPHY

Affleck, Diane Fagan. *Just New From the Mills*. North Andover, Mass.: Museum of American Textile History, 1987.

Appleton, Nathan. *Introduction of the Power Loom and the Origin of Lowell*. Lowell: Printed for the Proprietors of the Locks and Canals on Merrimack River, 1858.

Armstrong, John Borden. *Factory Under the Elms: A History of Harrisville, New Hampshire, 1774–1969*. 2nd ed. North Andover, Mass.: Museum of American Textile History, 1985.

Bagnall, William R. *The Textile Industries of the United States . . .* Vol. I (1639–1810). Cambridge, Mass.: The Riverside Press, 1893.

Baines, Edward. *History of the Cotton Manufacture in Great Britain . . .* London: H. Fisher, 1835.

[Batchelder, Samuel.] *Introduction and Early Progress of the Cotton Manufacture in the United States*. Boston: Little, Brown, 1863.

Bishop, James Leander. *A History of American Manufactures from 1608–1860*. 2 vols. Philadelphia: Edward Young, 1861–64.

Bremmer, Robert E. *Children and Youth in America*. 2 vols. Cambridge, Mass.: Harvard University Press, 1970.

Candee, Richard. 1982. "Architecture and Corporate Planning in the Waltham System." *Essays from the Lowell Conference on Industrial History*, Robert Weible, ed. North Andover, Mass.: Museum of American Textile History, 1985.

Clark, Victor S. *History of Manufactures in the United States*. 3 vols. New York: Published for the Carnegie Institution by McGraw-Hill, 1929.

Cole, Arthur H. *The American Wool Manufacture*. 2 vols. Cambridge, Mass.: Harvard University Press, 1926.

Cole, Donald B. *Immigrant City: Lawrence, Massachusetts, 1845–1921*. Chapel Hill: University of North Carolina Press, 1963.

Cole, J. R. *The History of Tolland, Connecticut . . .* New York: W. W. Preston & Co., 1888.

Dublin, Thomas. *Women at Work: The Transformation of Work and Community in Lowell, Massachusetts, 1826–1860*. New York: Columbia University Press, 1979.

Dunwell, Steve. *The Run of the Mill: A Pictorial Narrative of the Expansion, Dominion, Decline and Enduring Impact of the New England Textile Industry*. Boston: David R. Godine, 1978.

Fish, Carl Russell. *The Rise of the Common Man, 1830–1850*. New York: The Macmillan Company, 1927.

Gibb, George Sweet. *The Saco-Lowell Shops: Textile Machinery Building in New England, 1813–1949*. Cambridge, Mass.: Harvard University Press, 1939.

Greenleaf, Moses. *A Survey of the State of Maine . . .* Portland, Maine: Shirley & Hyde, 1829.

Gross, Lawrence F. *The Course of Industrial Decline: The Boott Cotton Mills of Lowell, Massachusetts, 1835–1955*. Baltimore: Johns Hopkins University Press, c. 1993.

Hanlan, James P. *The Working Population of Manchester, New Hampshire, 1840–1886*. Ann Arbor, Mich.: UMI Research Press/University Microfilms Intl., 1981.

Haraven, Tamara K. and Randolph Langenbach. *Amoskeag: Life and Work in an American Factory City*. New York: Pantheon Books, 1978.

Hayes, J. *History of the City of Lawrence*. Lawrence, Mass.: E. D. Green, 1868.

Hindle, Brooke, ed. *Material Culture in the Wooden Age*. Tarrytown, N.Y.: Sleepy Hollow Press, 1981.

Hough, Henry Beetle. *Wamsutta of New Bedford . . .* New Bedford, Mass.: The Vineyard Gazette, ed., 1946.

Hudon, Paul. *The Valley and Its People: An Illustrated History of the Lower Merrimack*. Woodland Hills, Calif.: Windsor, 1982.

Jeremy, David J. *Transatlantic Industrial Revolution: The Diffusion of Textile Technologies Between Britain and America, 1790–1830*. Cambridge, Mass.: M.I.T. Press; North Andover, Mass.: Merrimack Valley Textile Museum, 1981.

Knowlton, Evelyn H. *Pepperell's Progress: History of a Cotton Textile Company, 1844–1945*. Cambridge, Mass.: Harvard University Press, 1948.

Kulik, Gary, Roger Parks, and Theodore Z. Penn, eds. *The New England Mill Village, 1790–1860*. Cambridge,

Mass.: M.I.T. Press; North Andover, Mass.: Merrimack Valley Textile Museum, 1982.

Lawrence Up To Date, 1845–1895. Lawrence, Mass.: Rushforth & Donoghue, 1895.

Leavitt, Thomas W., ed. *The Hollingworth Letters: Technical Change in the Textile Industry, 1826–37.* Cambridge, Mass.: The Society for the History of Technology and M.I.T. Press, 1969.

Nash, Charles. *The History of Augusta.* Augusta, Maine: Charles E. Nash & Sons, 1904.

Navin, Thomas R. *The Whitin Machine Works Since 1831: A Textile Machinery Company in an Industrial Village.* Cambridge, Mass.: Harvard University Press, 1950.

Prude, Jonathan. *The Coming of the Industrial Order: Town and Factory Life in Rural Massachusetts, 1810–1860.* Cambridge: Cambridge University Press, 1983.

Potter, Chandler E. *The History of Manchester . . .* Manchester, N.H.: C. E. Potter, 1856.

Richardson, E[rastus]. *History of Woonsocket.* Woonsocket, R.I.: S. S. Foss, 1876.

Rivard, Paul E. *The Home Manufacture of Cloth, 1790–1840.* Pawtucket, R.I.: Slater Mill Historic Site, 1974.

Steere, Thomas. *History of the Town of Smithfield . . .* Providence: E. L. Freeman & Co., 1881.

Taylor, George Rogers. *The Transportation Revolution, 1815–1860.* New York: Harper & Row, 1951.

Tocqueville, Alexis de. *Democracy in America.* 2 vols. Boston: C. C. Little & J. Brown, 1841.

Ure, Andrew. *The Cotton Manufacture of Great Britain Investigated and Illustrated.* 2 vols. London: H. G. Bohn, 1861.

Ware, Caroline F. *The Early New England Cotton Manufacture: A Study in Industrial Beginnings.* Boston: Houghton Mifflin, 1931.

White, George S. *Memoir of Samuel Slater . . . with a History of the Rise and Progress of the Cotton Manufacture in England and America.* Philadelphia: Printed at 46 Carpenter St., 1836.

INDEX

Page numbers in italics refer to illustrations.

Textile industry (*continued*)
126–31. *See also* Domestic textile production; Factory textile production; Imported cloth; Textile machinery

Textile machinery: combing machines, 125; cotton comber, 141; Crompton's spinning mule, 12–13, *37*; jacks, 91, *91*, *92*, *93*; knitting machines, 85; mill and machine distinguished, 13, 51–52; new markets for, 141–44; new tools for domestic production, 19–26; obsolescence of New England's, 143–44; patents, 46, 135–37; power transmission, 53–54, 57, 58; roller printing presses, 66, 68, 71, 72; roller spinning frame, 8, 10, 11, 12; shearing machines, *84*; steam engines for, 126–31; technical innovations of 1760s, 8, 10–11; tending becoming more difficult, 113; throstle machines, 11, 72, *137*; waterpower for, 51–58; for woolen manufacturing, 81, 89–94. *See also* Carding machines; Looms; Machine shops; Spinning jenny

Textiles. *See* Cotton cloth; Linen; Woolen cloth

Thomas and Wilson company, 83

Thompson (Connecticut), 35, 53, 95

Thorpe, John, 46, 136

Throstle machines, 11, 72, *137*

Tocqueville, Alexis de, 98, 112, 116

Tow-cloth, 5, 31

Toweling, 32

Tow rope, 31

Tracy, Jedediah, 41, 43

Troy (Massachusetts). *See* Fall River

Turbines, 58, 113

Tyler v. Wilkinson, 54

Union Cotton and Woolen Manufactory (Manville, Connecticut), 108–9

Ure, Andrew, 108

Uxbridge (Massachusetts), *42*

Vertical spinning jenny, 25

Waltham (Massachusetts): Boston Associates building mills in, 44, 50; Boston Manufacturing Company mill in, *45*; power looms in, 22, 44; sheeting produced in, 46; success of cotton industry in, 32; the Waltham system, 49–50, *60*; women employed in, 98, 100, 102

Wamsutta Mills (New Bedford, Massachusetts), 129, *129*, 131

Ware (Massachusetts), 93, 97, 123, 135

War of 1812, 34

Warren (Rhode Island), 21

Washington Mills (Lawrence, Massachusetts), 125

Water frame (roller spinning frame), 8, 10, 11, 12

Waterpower, 51–58; competition for, 54–58; from New England rivers, 1–2; at Pawtucket, Rhode Island, 9; power looms requiring, 49; railroads fostering development of, 132–33; steam power replacing, 126–28; turbines, 58, 113. *See also* Waterwheels

Waterwheels: at Ashworth and Jones Mill, 56; improvements required in, 52–53; at Merrimack Manufacturing Company, 51; at Middlefield, New York, mill, 55; power transmission, 53–54

Weaving: mechanization of, 20; as women's work, 3. *See also* Hand weaving; Looms

Webster (Massachusetts), *36*, 47, 83, 87

Wheeler, Dexter, 129

White, George S., 14, 39

Whitin, John C., 139

Whitin, Paul, 139

Whitin Machine Company, 139, 141

Whitin's Improved Picker, 139

Whitin's Patent Pick & Spreader, *140*

Whitinsville (Massachusetts), 141

Whittier, John Greenleaf, 102, 111

Wilkinson, David: as better mechanic than businessman, 139; Killingly, Connecticut, mill of, 57; in power loom development, 46–47; Reynolds water frame improved by, 12; satinet produced by, 87; Slater and, 41; slide-rest lathe developed by, 136

Wilkinson, Oziel, Mill (Pawtucket, Rhode Island): breastwheel of, 52; built during "cotton mill fever," 41; contemporary photograph of, *38*; gearing at, 52; photograph of 1875, *38*, *39*, *41*; power transmission at, 53, 54; raceway for, *39*; water rights problems of, 54

Wilkinson, Smith, 14, 40–41, 96, 98

Williams, John, 72

Williams, T. A., 46

Willis, Nathaniel Parker, 126, 131

Winthrop (Maine), *104*

Women: advantages of mill work for, 100; boardinghouses for, 50, 64–65, 102–6, *103*, *105*, *109*; cloth manufacture as work of, 3; discontent among mill workers, 111–12, 114–16; doffer girls, 97; emancipation of "mill girls," 109; fashions, 78, *78*; Female Labor Reform Association, 114, 115, 116; flax spinning as work of, 30; in Lowell, Massachusetts, mills, 64–65, 100–101, 102, 109; as mill operatives, 95, 98–109; power looms operated by, 23, 98, 100; de Tocqueville on, 116; Waltham system employing, 50

Woolen cloth, 79–88; broadcloth, 79, 80, 83; carding machines come to New England, 15–18; cassimere, 83, 91–94; colonists bringing sheep to North America, 2; first documented woolen mill, 79; flannel, 7, 83–85; Franklin Mill samples of, 82; hand carding, 16; home production of, 15, 80; homespun cloth, 3; innovations in production of, 89–91; investment in mills for, 87; Knowles Fancy Loom for, *142*; linsey-woolsey, 86; machinery for, 81, 89–94; men in workforce, *80*; mixed cloth, 86; new tools for domestic production of, 23–26; satinet, 83, 86–87; small mills for, 87–88; the typical New England mill, 80–83; worsted, 124–25

Woonsocket (Rhode Island): Harris mills, 57, 112; labor conditions in, 98; Montgomery on mills in, 43; Reddy settling in, 118; six mill villages forming, 35; waterpower use in, 54

Woonsocket Falls, 35

Worcester (Massachusetts): Ashworth and Jones Mill, 56; Crompton and Knowles, 141, *142*, 143; Crompton Loom Works, *140*; home spinners and weavers near, 93–94; mill development in, 35; Phelps and Bickford, 92

Workers. *See* Mill workers

Worsted wool, 124–25

York Manufacturing Company (Saco, Maine), 43, *61*, 106, 143